Sept 9, 2012

To

South Bend First Brethren Church,
partners in Malaysia + cl........ sions,

" May you be blessed in reading
this book."

love + blessings,
David + Jenny Loi

*"This book contains truth that will make you free
and able to fulfill your 'Call to Sonship'."* - Dr Bill Hamon.

BILLY C.S. WONG

Foreword
by Dr. Bill Hamon

Billy Wong has done a tremendous job of bringing clarity and revelation of humanity becoming sons of God. The reader will develop a greater knowledge and ability to become a true son of God in this day and hour. Every believer is called to sonship but not all believers grow to become mature sons of God who can become colaborers with Christ Jesus.

This book contains truth that will make you free and able to fulfill your 'Call to Sonship'. Bless you Brother Wong for allowing God to work in your life to bring revelation and transformation that has enabled you to write this book.

Every Christian needs to read this book.

Bill Hamon

Dr. Bill Hamon
Founder and Bishop: Christian International Ministries
Apostle and Prophet: Christian International Apostolic Network (CIAN)
Author of 10 major books including, "The Eternal Church" and "The Day Of The Saints"

Dedication

This book is dedicated to our Lord Jesus Christ, who revealed Himself to me in prophetic dreams and charged me through prophetic words to write *The Sons of God* series. I am not a prolific writer and should be the last of all to undertake this work. Yet it is His good pleasure to set me apart (even when I was in my mother's womb) and to give me the privilege to undertake this divine assignment of writing for the purpose of revealing God's eternal purpose and the Father's heart's desire. To Him I offer my heartfelt thanks for helping me throughout the course of my writing.

This book is also dedicated to the many redeemed, regenerated, now being transformed, and soon to be glorified sons of God all over the world. I pray that whoever read it will run with the visions and will get ready to hasten the return of our Firstborn Brother, our Bridegroom, the Lamb-God, the King of kings, and the Lord of lords.

Preface

In 1990, I was in my final year towards completing an accounting degree in Victoria University of Wellington, New Zealand. In a church camp that same year, a man of God handpicked me from the crowd, laid his hand upon me and gave me these prophetic words:

"Brother, the Lord wants to release to you a special calling of leadership; a mantle of leadership shall come upon you and you shall recognize it and know it and run with it. You will not in any way waver because of that call. For behold, says the Lord, it is a vast and expansive vision that I will open up to you, my son, and I will cause you to find that vision growing step by step and piece by piece and as you are able to understand and handle each phase I shall open up the next phase to you, says the Lord. And so it shall be until the vision is completed.

Be not frustrated. Look not at your own inabilities, your own limitations, says God, for I have called you. You have recognized the calling that is upon your life and you have responded to that call. Therefore I have come to encourage you this day to let me be the Lord. Let me again stir within you, my servant, that call which is upon your life. Let it come from deep within your spirit, says God, for that which I have laid upon you is a large and heavy burden but it shall be that which comes by my Spirit, says the Lord your God."

This book, *The Call to Sonship*, the first of "the Sons of God" series, is part of that "vast and expansive vision" that the Lord has given me. As you read this book prayerfully, may the Lord use the truths and principles presented in this volume to quicken your spirit, renew your heart, and challenge your mind to respond to God's call for your life - the call to sonship.

To God be the glory both now and forever! Amen.

Billy C. S. Wong

Contents

PART 2: THE DIVINE DISPENSATION

ADDENDUM

THE S●NS
OF G●D
S E R I E S

Part 1

The Call to Sonship

Part 1

The Call to Sonship

The Earth School of Preparation

Let me begin by sharing an ancient story. Once upon a time, a mighty king ruled over the whole earth. One day, there was a big celebration throughout the land. The reason for rejoicing: a prince was born who was destined to sit on the throne and be the appointed heir to his father's kingdom.

The wise king, being near his advanced age, eagerly desired that the prince would one day become the next king to rule over the earth. Before this could happen, he must wait for the prince, who was merely a child, to grow into maturity as a son and be thoroughly prepared so that he would possess all the virtues and attributes of a good king. The prince was born by this purpose and for this purpose, and all the preparations in his life were to enable him to fulfill his father's purpose for him.

The king thus called a matron to send the newborn child into a village to be nursed and cared for by one of the appointed village folks. Unaware of his true identity as a prince, the boy grew up in the village and lived an ordinary life. He did not realize that his community life was under the king's noble and thoughtful arrangement in order to shape him for future greatness. All the people, matters and circumstances that the prince encountered in his daily living were neither accidents nor coincidences, but were instrumental in bringing him to a place of maturity and adulthood. In other words, the providential arrangement of the circumstances surrounding the prince was designed for the purpose of maturing him as a son and qualifying him as the legal heir. The prince was in training for rulership — his sufferings were intended for his welfare, promotion, and glory.

From the villagers' point of view, having such an unusual arrangement — to raise the prince in a village rather than allowing him to grow up in the palace — was seemingly unfair. The challenges and hardships that the prince would have to endure were unnecessary. If he had been raised in the palace, he would have had many privileges and many servants to attend to him. However, from the king's perspective, the present hard times and sufferings experienced by the prince were nothing compared to the great glory which was about to be unfolded and revealed to him. For it was the purposeful determination of the king to raise the prince for glory and not for shame, for honor and not humiliation, for victory and not defeat.

Finally, the years of preparations were over and the boy grew up to be a matured man with good characteristics and virtues. When the king was informed that the prince had come to full age of maturity and perfection of character, the king, out of his love, sent the matron to bring the prince back into the palace. However, his adopted family and the village people wept for the departure of the prince from among them. Yet one wise man said to them: "Why do you weep? Was this not the king's son, whose true place is in his father's palace, and not with you?"

This story gives us a glimpse of why we were born into this planet. We are placed on this earth by God in order to fulfill His purpose for our lives. In fact, this earth is a school of preparation so that we might fulfill God's eternal purpose for the human race. If you have been constantly asking yourself, "What on earth am I here for?", you must now discover the purpose of your existence. This book invites you to begin the journey of discovering God's unique purpose for your life.

This earth is like a village or a school for every child of God. The Earth School prepares you to fulfill God's eternal purpose for you — to be His sons and legal heirs. The curriculum in the Earth School is the same for every believer in Christ: Divine Sonship. Like any other school on earth, there are classes that you must attend and lessons that you must learn as a student in this Earth school. When you have completed the assigned classes, you are given the opportunity to advance to other classes. There is only one teacher in the Earth School — the Indwelling life-giving Spirit. From the day that you were born in the spirit, He enrolled you into certain classes until you have learnt the lessons. These lessons are designed to change and transform you, to bring you into maturity as the sons of God so that you might be prepared to become the future kings of the earth and legal heirs of the kingdom of God.

The Bible tells us plainly, "No eye has seen, no ear has heard, no mind has conceived what God has prepared for those who love him" (1 Co.2:9 NIV). Regardless of how you think and feel about God as a believer at this point in your life, God is progressively unfolding the mystery of His will to you and is inviting you to participate in His divine plan so that He can bring into completion the good work He has begun in you. Your life is under His purposeful arrangement and He doesn't want you to miss out on His wonderful plan for your life. You were born for such a time as this and you must pass all the tests of the Earth school to fully prepare yourself for the coming grand graduation or coronation. Those who have successfully graduated from the Earth school shall be the sons of God, qualified as the legal heirs of the Father's kingdom, ruling and reigning with His Son — Jesus — as co-kings in the coming Millennium Age.

So, like the ancient wise king, God in His divine wisdom is preparing His children for the fulfillment of His eternal purpose — to bring us into full sonship so that we might be co-heirs of Christ and co-kings with Christ for the ultimate expression and manifestation of God's glory throughout eternity. Today, we are sons and kings in the making — God is placing us in the Earth School or the School of Sonship where the lessons are taught for the working out of His perfect will for our lives.

The serious question you must now ponder upon is this: God's plan includes you, but does your plan include God? We must choose wisely today to walk in God's plan and to invite God to work in us for the accomplishment of His eternal purpose for our lives.

The Lord Jesus as the Prototype of the Sons of God

The ancient story might have also reminded you of the life of the Lord Jesus Christ while He was on this earth two thousand years ago. Although He was the eternal Son of God, He made Himself nothing, taking the very nature of a servant and appearing in human form. He was born in a manger, raised as a carpenter's son in a small town called Capernaum, and at the age of 30 he was ready to fulfill the mission entrusted to Him by God the Father. After He had accomplished His earthly mission through His suffering and ultimate death on the cross, He descended to the Hades, rose on the third day, ascended to heaven and became the appointed heir of all things (Heb.1:2). The Book of Philippians describes Him in this way:

> *Philippians 2:5-11 KJV*
> *Let this mind be in you, which was also in Christ Jesus: Who, being in the form of God, thought it not robbery to be equal with God: But made himself of no reputation, and took upon him the form of a servant, and was made in the likeness of men: And being found in fashion as a man, he humbled himself, and became obedient unto death, even the death of the cross. Wherefore God also hath highly exalted him, and given him a name which is above every name: That at the name of Jesus every knee should bow, of things in heaven, and things in earth, and things under the earth; And that every tongue should confess that Jesus Christ is Lord, to the glory of God the Father.*

The phrase "Let this mind be in you, which was also in Christ Jesus" reminds us that we must have the same attitude and purpose to cherish the same view as that of the Lord Jesus

Christ concerning our lives on earth. We are to learn from Him and take after His pattern of suffering on our earthly journeys. The Bible tells us that Christ as the Firstborn is a prototype and a pattern of many brothers who is to be conformed to His image (Rom.8:29). To start our preparation in the Earth School, we must first take the Lord Jesus as the role model in the journey of our lives. We are to fix our eyes on Jesus, the author and perfector of our faith, and behold Him for ourselves so that inwardly we might be transformed into His image with ever-increasing glory and become more and more like Him (Heb. 12:2; 2 Co.3:18). Ultimately, when He appears in His second coming, we shall be glorified to be like Him in His bodily likeness (1 John 3:2). When we graduate from the Earth School, we shall all be the sons of God, Christ's many brothers, the same as He is, in image and likeness, in life and nature, in expression and constitution.

The Book of Hebrews further describes that the character and manhood of Jesus were made perfect through His earthly suffering and thus He becomes the author of salvation to bring many sons to glory.

> *Hebrews 2:10-11 NIV*
> *In bringing many sons to glory, it was fitting that God, for whom and through whom everything exists, should make the author of their salvation perfect through suffering. Both the one who makes men holy and those who are made holy are of the same family. So Jesus is not ashamed to call them brothers.*

To be the Pioneer, Leader, Author of our salvation and the Sanctifier of many brothers, Christ must first undergo human sufferings to qualify Him as the Firstborn of these many brothers. For the believers to be brought into the same estate as God's glorified sons, we must take after the pattern of Christ in our experience with human sufferings and allow the Lord to bring us through all the necessary processes that would mould and transform us to become God's true sons. God's methods of bringing us into maturity often involve His discipline and chastisement through trials, sufferings and afflictions. These are the lessons that we must learn in the Earth School and tests that we must pass in order to undergo an inner transformation to be made conformable to the image of Christ the Firstborn — the Prototype of the many sons of God. The writer of Hebrews spoke directly and emphatically about God disciplining His children so that they might be partakers of His holy nature to become His true sons:-

> *Hebrews 12:5-11 AMP*
> *And have you [completely] forgotten the divine word of appeal and encouragement in which you are reasoned with and addressed as sons? My son, do not think lightly or scorn to submit to the correction and discipline of the Lord, nor lose courage and give up and faint when you are reproved or corrected by Him; For the Lord corrects and disciplines everyone whom He loves, and He punishes, even scourges, every son whom He accepts and welcomes to His heart and cherishes. You must submit to and endure [correction] for discipline; God is dealing with you as with sons. For what son is there whom his father does not [thus] train and correct and discipline? Now if you are exempt from correction and left without discipline in which all [of God's children] share, then you are illegitimate offspring and not true sons [at all].Moreover, we have had earthly fathers who disciplined us and we yielded [to them] and respected [them for training us]. Shall we not much more cheerfully submit to the Father of spirits and so [truly] live? For [our earthly fathers] disciplined us for only a short period of time and chastised us as seemed proper and good to them; but He disciplines us for our certain good, that we may become sharers in His own holiness. For the time being no discipline brings joy, but seems grievous*

and painful; but afterwards it yields a peaceable fruit of righteousness to those who have been trained by it [a harvest of fruit which consists in righteousness--in conformity to God's will in purpose, thought, and action, resulting in right living and right standing with God].

As noted earlier, the many sons of God are the many brothers of Christ while Christ Himself is the Firstborn among many brothers. God's deepest desire is to raise a family with many sons who are partakers of His own life and nature and sharers of Christ's glory, rulership and dominion. Concerning this, Paul E. Billheimer made a truly remarkable assertion of Christ as the Prototype of the many sons of God:

> *Those who have worked on an assembly line know that a prototype is first designed, handcrafted, and tested before it is committed to the assembly line. They also know that the purpose of the assembly line is to produce exact duplicates, perfect copies of the original. This is God's purpose in the plan of redemption - to produce, by means of the new birth, an entirely new and unique species, exact replicas of His Son with whom He will share His glory and His dominion, and who will constitute a royal progeny and form the governing and administrative staff of His eternal kingdom.*

> *While we recognize the infinite distinction between the Eternal Son and the "many sons" born into the family, yet such is their heredity as the result of the new birth that He recognizes them as bona fide blood-brothers. And according to 1 John 3:2 that is just what they are, true genetic sons of God and therefore blood-brothers of the Son. Christ is the divine Prototype after which this new species is being made. They are to be exact copies of Him, true genotypes, as utterly like Him as it is possible for the finite to be like the infinite. As sons of God, begotten by Him, incorporating into their fundamental being and nature the very "genes" of God, they rank*

above all other created beings and are elevated to the most sublime height possible short of becoming members of the Trinity itself. Although Christ is the unique and only begotten Eternal Son, yet He does not retain His glory for Himself alone for He has declared, "The glory which thou gavest me, I have given them" (John 17:22). Therefore, the redeemed will share His glory, His rulership, and His dominion as truly responsible princes of the Realm.[1]

The insight here regarding the divine sonship of believers is genuine and revelatory, worthy of our affirmation. As we shall see later, a proper and balanced understanding of sonship will lead us to a richer and more profound experience of the organic work of God in the believer, thus enabling us to progressively mature in the divine life to attain to our full inheritance as sons of God through Christ.

There are two important laws of sonship. The first one is "perfecting through suffering" and the other is "maturing by assimilating the divine life". Even though God can use sufferings and afflictions as means of conforming us to the image of Christ, His primary way to progressively transform us is by the work of the Indwelling Spirit within the believers. It is the operation and inner working of the Indwelling Spirit that form and shape our inner beings with the divine life and nature so that believers are ultimately transformed inwardly to be the same as Christ is, in life and nature, in expression and constitution. The sons of God are produced by the organic work of the Indwelling Spirit — filling, saturating and permeating our whole being with the life of God. Nevertheless, the outward pressure, trials and afflictions can often be instrumental in bringing us to closer walk and deeper intimacy with God. It is by our Christ-like endurance of earthly sufferings and our obedience to the Indwelling Spirit together with our cooperation with Him to experience His organic work within us that can genuinely bring about a progressive and real inward transformation so that we become more and more like Christ our Prototype and ultimately, our glorification as the sons of God — the completion of God's goal of salvation.

Predestination unto Sonship

G od's eternal plan and purpose is to gain many divine sons for the satisfaction of His heart's desire. Who are these many sons? They are the redeemed, regenerated, transformed and glorified humanity. This concept of sonship is presented clearly by Apostle Paul in Ephesians 1, where he set out man's salvation from God's perspective:-

> *Ephesians 1:3-10 NIV (emphasis mine)*
> *Praise be to the God and Father of our Lord Jesus Christ, who has blessed us in the heavenly realms with every spiritual blessing in Christ. For he chose us in him before the creation of the world to be holy and blameless in his sight.* **In love he predestined us to be adopted as his sons through Jesus Christ, in accordance with his pleasure and will** *— to the praise of his glorious grace, which he has freely given us in the One he loves. In him we have redemption through his blood, the forgiveness of sins, in accordance with the riches of God's grace that he lavished on us with all wisdom and understanding. And he made known to us the mystery of his will according to his good pleasure, which he purposed in Christ, to be put into effect when the times will have reached their fulfillment – to bring all things in heaven and on earth together under one head, even Christ.*

Kenneth Wuest translated verses 4-5 as:

> *"..even as He selected us out for himself in Him before the foundations of the universe were laid, to be holy ones and without blemish before His searching, penetrating gaze; in love having previously marked us out to be placed as adult sons through the intermediate agency of Jesus Christ for himself according to which seemed*

good in His heart's desire."[2]

Rotherham translated verse 5 as *"In love marking us out beforehand unto sonship, through Jesus Christ, for himself, according to the good pleasure of his will."*[3] Thus, it is most important to note that the concept of divine sonship is the very central and purpose of God's plan for humanity and we must therefore not regard it as a trivial matter. Sonship is **THE PURPOSE** because it is *"according to the good pleasure of his will."* "Good pleasure" because nothing pleases God more than divine sonship, for it is His eternal delight, satisfaction and purpose. God's will is sonship — nothing more, nothing less, and nothing else. The word "will" in Greek is *thelema*, *"a desire which proceeds from one's heart and emotion"*. Paul pointed out that sonship is *"the mystery of His will according to His good pleasure."* A divine mystery is a secret that is hidden or unknown to human reasoning and can only be made known by the revelation of God. This mystery is God's will according to His good pleasure. God's will is God's eternal plan and purpose which proceed out of the good pleasure of His heart. According to God's eternal plan and purpose for the satisfaction of His heart's desire, He predestined us unto sonship.

The subject of predestination has caused a great deal of debate in the Christian church for centuries because of the general lack of crucial understanding concerning the purpose of God's predestination. Ephesians 1:5 makes it clear that predestination is unto sonship. *"Unto"*, *eis*, is a preposition which means *"with a view to"*, signifying purpose or result. *Predestinate* in Greek is *proorizo*, derived from *pro*, *"before"* and *horizo*, *"to mark out the boundaries or limits and hence to determine, to ordain"*. When applied to persons, it means *"to put limitations upon that person"*, thus *"to determine his destiny"*. Predestination, *proorizo*, therefore connotes the idea of ownership — that someone was predestined, foreordained, predetermined and marked out beforehand by another person with a view that he could be owned and possessed by the one who sets the limit upon him. However, the focus here is not who the objects of this predestination are, but what they are predestined for. Predestination is unto a purpose, and this purpose is sonship.

Besides introducing the important concept of divine sonship being God's eternal purpose for the created human race according to His predestination for the good pleasure of His will, Paul in the Book of Romans gave further insights into the various steps of God's saving plan in which He gains the fallen human race to become His glorified sons:-

> *Romans 8:28-30 KJV*
> *And we know that all things work together for good to them that love God, to them who are called according to his purpose. For whom he did foreknow, he also did predestinate to be conformed to the image of his Son, that he might be the firstborn among many brethren. Moreover whom he did predestinate, them he also called; and whom he called, them he also justified: and whom he justified, them he also glorified.*

Here, Paul not only links predestination with God's purpose, but also qualifies that predestination based on God's foreknowledge: *"for whom he did foreknow, he also did predestinate"*. From this foreknowledge, God chose us in Christ before the foundation of the world (Eph.1:4). The word *choose* in Greek is *eklegomai* from *ek* "out" and *lego* "to speak". Spiros Zodhiates defined *eklegomai* as

> *"To speak intelligently. To choose, select, choose for oneself, not necessarily implying the rejection of what is not chosen but giving favor to the chosen subject, keeping in view a relation to be established between him and the object. It involves selection and choice from among many."*[4]

Therefore, God's selection and appointment is for the attainment of a certain objective and goal, and that objective and goal is sonship.

We must reject the erroneous idea that predestination connotes the notion of eternal perdition of the unsaved, for God does not want anyone to perish but all to come to repentance (2 Pe.3:9). Predestination was never meant for eternal perdition, but always with a view of conforming the called one to God's saving purpose, which is sonship. For the fulfillment of this eternal purpose of sonship, God chose us in Christ by marking us out and picking us out from among the countless people of the earth. He chose us by calling us by name in order to invite us to participate in the blessings of salvation. Thus, *"whom he did predestinate, them he also called"*.

These blessings of salvation provided for the called ones include justification, transformation and glorification. The called one becomes the justified one through redemption by the blood of Christ. The justified one must then go through the process of transformation to conform to the image of Christ to become the transformed one and the complete transformation will eventually bring forth the glorified one. Hence, *"and whom he called, them he also justified: and whom he justified, them he also glorified."*

The Amplified Bible expounds Romans 8:30 as:
> *"And those whom he thus foreordained, He also called; and those whom He called, He also justified (acquitted, made righteous, putting them into right standing with Himself). And those whom He justified, He also glorified [raising them to a heavenly dignity and condition or state of being]."*

God's work of salvation upon us began with His foreknowing and predestination, followed by His calling and justification and ending in glorification. Glorification is thus the completion, the consummation and the full attainment of the divine sonship. God desires to bring many sons into glory (Heb.2:10). He calls us into glory and we are to be transformed from glory to glory (2 Co.3:18). He will ultimately glorify us at the coming of the Lord by transfiguring the body of our humble state into conformity with the body of His glory (Phil.3:21).

The following chart summarizes the various stages and progressions of the outworking of God's salvation plan for the fulfillment of His eternal plan and purpose to bring us into full sonship so that we might become the manifested sons of God, reigning with Christ in the New Millennium and consummating as the Bride, the Wife of the Lamb and the New Jerusalem in the eternity future.

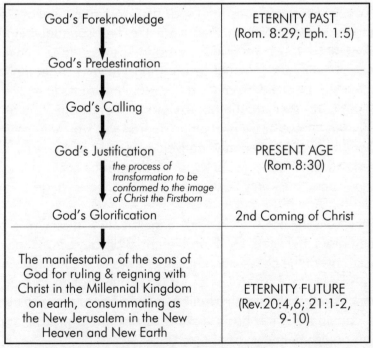

God's Foreknowledge ↓ God's Predestination	ETERNITY PAST (Rom. 8:29; Eph. 1:5)
↓ God's Calling ↓ God's Justification *the process of transformation to be conformed to the image of Christ the Firstborn* ↓ God's Glorification	PRESENT AGE (Rom.8:30) 2nd Coming of Christ
↓ The manifestation of the sons of God for ruling & reigning with Christ in the Millennial Kingdom on earth, consummating as the New Jerusalem in the New Heaven and New Earth	ETERNITY FUTURE (Rev.20:4,6; 21:1-2, 9-10)

God's Eternal Plan and Purpose for Man – Sonship

Various Usages of "Son" or "Sons" of God in the Bible

For a greater understanding of the crucial element of sonship in God's purpose, we must closely examine the five different biblical usages of "son" or "sons" of God in both the Old and New Testaments.

a) The Angels as the Sons of God
The angels were called *bene ha-elohim* or "sons of God" six times in the Old Testament: three times in the book of Job (Job 1:6; 2:1; 38:7), twice in the book of Psalms (Ps.29:1; 89:6) and once in Genesis 6:2.[5]

The appellation "sons of God" was assigned initially to angels simply because they were the first spiritual beings created by God. As supra-terrestrial beings, they derived their angelic life (created, everlasting life with a beginning but without an end) from God. Living in the immediate circle of the Lord, they are the objects of His special affection and concern. These heavenly beings guard God's throne, praise God, fight God's enemy, deliver messages to humans, or perform other services for God. Other terms such as "holy ones" and "heavenly host" are also assigned to angels.

After humankind was created, angels play a major role as mediators between God and men. Biblical records gave accounts of the active and important roles of angels in giving themselves to the services of God for ministration to men's needs and for the administration of God's dealings with men in carrying out the basic tasks of proclamation, protection and punishment.

In contrast to the Old Testament, angels were never designated as "sons of God" in the New Testament. The Greek word for "angel" is *aggelos*, which means "a messenger" or "one who is sent". Hebrews 1:14, in particular, addressed angels as the "ministering spirits sent to service those who will inherit salvation".

b) The People of Israel as God's Son
The image of filiation was used in the Old Testament for expressing God's paternal affection for the people of Israel. In numerous occasions, God addressed Israel with the title of "son". Such an instance can be found in Exodus 4:22 when God commanded Moses to speak to Pharaoh: "Israel is my firstborn son, let my son go, so he may worship me." God's love for Israel was also expressed in Hosea 11:1: "When Israel was a child, I loved him, and out of Egypt I called my son." Speaking to all the people, Moses reminded the Israelites: "You are the sons of the LORD your God... For you are a people holy to the LORD your God, and the LORD has chosen you to be a people for his own possession, out of all the peoples that are on the face of the earth" (Dt.14:1-2 ASV).

The metaphor of the word "son" is sometimes replaced by the image of the "spouse" (in particular in the oracles of Hosea) to express the covenant relationship between God and Israel. The people of Israel were known as "son" or "spouse" by God because God has chosen them to be His own and was responsible to guide and protect them. In return for God's faithfulness, the people of Israel were to set themselves apart as God's chosen people and to serve Jehovah God alone. More importantly, the people of Israel have a special place in the heart of God because they were instrumental to the birthing of Christ, the only begotten Son of God, into the world.

c) Chosen Individuals as God's "Son"

Some individuals who were chosen by God to act as appointed judges and kings on His behalf to rule the nation of Israel — to judge and deal with the enemies of the Israelites — were also honored by God with the title of "son". In Psalms 82:6-7, addressing the wicked judges who failed to act righteously, God declared: "I said, 'you are "gods"; you are all sons of the Most High. But you will die like mere men; you will fall like every other ruler." In the cases of David and Solomon, God showed his paternal affections to them when God spoke about David: "He will call out to me, 'You are my father, my God, the Rock my Savior.' I will also appoint him my firstborn, the most exalted of the kings of the earth" (Ps.89:26-27). A similar promise was made concerning Solomon: "I will be his father, and he will be my son" (2 Sam.7:14).

This title of "son" was conferred by God on kings and judges because God granted them privileges and vested them with authority to act on His behalf to render justice on earth. Particularly for King David and Solomon, God's promises to them were also messianic in nature as they would prophetically point to Christ as the Firstborn Son of God and also the coming King to rule the earth in the Millennium Kingdom.[6]

d) Christ as the Son of God

It is significant to note that the Lord Jesus Christ was never referred to as a child of God as believers are in the New Testament. The term child was used to refer to Him only when He was a child growing up (Mt.2:8 Lk. 1:80). Jesus always asserted and affirmed Himself as the Son of God, the Messiah.

It is important for us to draw a clear distinction between

Christ as the unique and only Eternal Son of God (John 1:14, 18; 3:16, 18; 1 John 4:9) and Christ as the Firstborn Son of God (Rom.8:29; Col.1:15, 18; Heb.1:6). By virtue of His eternal existence in the Godhead, He is the only eternal Son of God. This eternal sonship in the Godhead is unique to Him and cannot be shared with anyone. Even prior to His incarnation, He was already the Son of God in His divinity. However, it was by incarnation that He put on a new element of humanity. Hence, He was the God - Man, fully divine yet fully human. He was the Son of God and yet the Son of Man at the same time. The Son of God refers to His divinity while the Son of Man refers to His humanity. Thus, being the Word made flesh, the Man Jesus had the divinity dwelling in His humanity — for in Christ all the fullness of the Deity lives in bodily form (Col.2:9) and God was pleased to have all His fullness dwell in him (Col.1:19).

The Lord Jesus was designated as the firstborn Son of God in His resurrected humanity, whereby He became the firstborn among many brothers. This divine begetting as the Firstborn Son of God fulfilled the messianic prophecy concerning Christ in Psalms 2:7, "He said to Me: 'You are My Son, Today I have begotten You.'" Paul also spoke of Christ's resurrection as God's begetting Him in Acts 13:33. Christ's own words after His resurrection was "Go instead to my brothers and tell them, `I am returning to my Father and your Father, to my God and your God.'" (John 20:17). Prior to His resurrection, the most intimate way the Lord called His disciples was "friends" (John 15:14-15). But after His resurrection, He could call the disciples "brothers" for the very first time because he was now designated as "the Firstborn among many brothers" and "the Firstborn from the dead" (Rom.8:29; Col.1:18; Rev.1:5). It was through His resurrection from the dead that His humanity was uplifted and divinized to become the Firstborn Son of God. As the

Firstborn Son, He is now the prototype and model of the many sons of God.

e) The Believers in Christ as the Sons of God
Positionally, all believers in Christ are called the sons of God (2 Co.6:18, Gal.3:26, 4:6; 1 Th. 5:5; Heb.12:5, 7).[7] However, we must clearly distinguish between believers as the sons of God and Christ as the Son of God. Believers are sons of God by virtue of their sharing of Christ's communicable attribute i.e. His divine life and nature.

As the eternal Son of God, Christ possesses both the communicable (dispensable) and incommunicable (indispensable) attributes of God. The communicable (dispensable) divine attribute is the divine life and nature of God which include His holiness, righteousness, love, joy and peace. The incommunicable (indispensable) attribute is what makes God uniquely God. The Bible reveals that the incommunicable and personal Name of God is Yahweh[8], which means "I am that I am" or "I will become whatsoever I may become". By virtue of being God, only He can declare: "I am the self existing One. I am the External God. I am the all sufficient God. I am omnipotent (All Powerful), I am omnipresent (All-present, present everywhere at the same time) and I am omniscient (All knowing, All seeing, I see and know all things at the same time). I was here in the past, I am here now, and I will be here in the future. I am the beginning and I am the end." This incommunicable Name signifies the incommunicable character, attributes and capacity of God that are reserved to Him alone as His sole privilege and right. It is by possessing this incommunicable attribute that qualifies Christ as the Godhead and in equality with God (Jn.17:11; Phil.2:6).

Believers are sons of God because they are sharers and participants of God's communicable attributes, thus possessing His life and nature (2 Pe. 1:4). When Christ underwent the process of death and resurrection, He became the Firstborn among many brothers. Now, as the Life Giving Spirit, He dispenses God's communicable attributes into those who believe in Him. Being the Firstborn Brother, Christ is the image and prototype that we must conform to so that we might be the same as He is, in life and in nature.

However, believers can never be the sharers of Christ's incommunicable attributes which qualify Him as the Godhead and sole Object of worship. Besides being our Firstborn brother, Christ also has a name written on Him which no one knows except Himself (Rev.19:12); and this unutterable Name which is personal to Christ speaks of His incommunicable character, attributes and capacity that are reserved for Him alone. Therefore, if we can draw a clear distinction between the communicable and the incommunicable attributes of God, we will be able to comprehend and appreciate that we will never become the same as Christ as the eternal Son of God since we can never possess the incommunicable divine attributes which God alone possesses. However, we can and will be the same as Christ the Firstborn in possessing the communicable attributes of God's life and nature.

Thus the term "sons of God" refers to believers whose humanity is sanctified, divinized, uplifted, and brought into sonship to be like Christ the Firstborn, conforming to His image and likeness, possessing God's life and nature (dispensable/communicable attributes of God).

All in all, whether the designation "son" or "sons" applies to angels, the people of Israel or some privileged chosen ones or the New Testaments believers depends on the strictness of its usage. As far as the people of Israel were concerned, the analogy of the divine filiation seemed to express a rather external relationship. Based on the covenant relationship, God demonstrated his paternal role toward Israel as their protector, provider and savior. However, this relationship between God and Israel (or other chosen ones) as "father-and-son" was merely external, for there was no genuine begetting to qualify them as the partakers of God's life and nature. This divine filiation was only a metaphor and a shadow of the good things to come (Heb.10:1). The very reality is the actual begetting of men to become the spiritual offspring of God through the divine birth — for "that which is born of the flesh is flesh, and that which is born of the Spirit is spirit" (Jn.3:6).

Various Definitions of the Word "Son" in the Bible

The word "son" carries four main denotations in the Bible. Firstly, in the Semitic language especially, it is a standard usage for expressing any relationship of belonging or a relationship to someone. It is usually used to designate a male offspring of parents. For instance, Christ is called the Son of David (Mt.1:1) to indicate that He was a genuine descendent of David.

Secondly, the term "son" is commonly used to indicate a quality or characteristic possessed by someone. For instance, the expression "son of peace" is used to describe the quality of peace possessed by that person. Christ is referred to as the Son of God (Jn. 5:25; 9:35; 10:36; 11:4) and the Son of Man (Lk.9:22, 12:8; Jn.1:51). While Son of God refers to Christ as a divine being possessing the nature and quality of divinity, Son of Man speaks of Christ as a human being possessing the nature and quality of humanity. Both designations indicate Christ as possessing the quality of a God-Man, having both the divine and human natures.

Thirdly, the term "son" carries the meaning of **someone who has been begotten of, generated, or descended from the begetter, having the same life and nature as he is.** Therefore the more accurate usage of the word "son" must imply either a natural birth or a divine birth by which something has been transmitted genetically from the begetter to produce the child. In light of this, anyone who calls himself a "son of God" must be genuinely begotten by God to have the same life and nature as He is.[9] Under this strict definition, angels or human beings are disqualified as genuine "son" or "sons" of God — for an angel possesses only the angelic life and a human being the human life. A son of God is a human being who possesses the divine life in addition to his human life.

Lastly, the term "son" indicates **the attainment of maturity** and deals particularly with **the rights to inheritance**. In ancient times, a son could only possess his father's inheritance when he was of full age. In the like manner, when believers attain maturity in life as full grown sons of God, they shall be qualified as heirs to inherit all that God is and has for them.

The concept of sonship for the fulfillment of God's eternal purpose incorporates both the notions of the **divine birth** and the **divine growth** for the attainment of full sonship. Believers are matured sons of God when they are regenerated in spirit, transformed in soul and glorified in body, thus possessing God's life and nature and conforming themselves to the image and likeness of Christ the Firstborn.

Children of God versus Sons of God

In order to fully appreciate the significance of sonship and respond heartily to God's divine call to sonship, it is important for us to draw a clear distinction between the term "children of God" and "sons of God". The New Testament clearly speaks of both *children of God* and *sons of God* and reveals their distinctions. Therefore, we must not confound that which God has carefully distinguished in His words.

Apostle Paul had a divine revelation and clear understanding concerning God's eternal purpose of gaining many sons. Hence, he made a clear distinction in his writings between *children of God* and *sons of God*. Unfortunately, many Bible translations overlooked the crucial element of sonship in God's purpose and thus failed to translate accurately the Greek word for *children* and *sons* by using them indistinguishably and interchangeably, obscuring the meaning between them.[10] By obliterating the God's revealed distinction between *children of God* and *sons of God*, the crucial understanding of biblical truth concerning sonship is lost. Furthermore, it forfeits the believers' rights and privileges to participate and cooperate with God for the attainment of sonship, which consequently, frustrates God's purpose to produce the many sons for the satisfaction of His heart's desire.

The study of two important Greek words pertaining to *children* and *sons* will bring to greater light the importance of this divine truth.

Romans 8:14-21 NIV
Because those who are led by the Spirit of God are
sons [huiós] of God. For you did not receive a spirit that
makes you a slave again to fear, but you received the
Spirit of sonship. And by him we cry, "Abba, Father." The
Spirit himself testifies with our spirit that we are God's
children [téknon]. Now if we are children [téknon], then
we are heirs--heirs of God and co-heirs with Christ,
if indeed we share in his sufferings in order that we
may also share in his glory. I consider that our present
sufferings are not worth comparing with the glory that
will be revealed in us. The creation waits in eager
expectation for the sons [huiós] of God to be revealed.
For the creation was subjected to frustration, not by its
own choice, but by the will of the one who subjected
it, in hope that the creation itself will be liberated from
its bondage to decay and brought into the glorious
freedom of the children [téknon] of God.

Dr Spiros Zodhiates made a helpful analysis of the distinction
between the two:

The difference between believers as children (tékna)
of God and as sons (huiós) is brought out in Romans
8:14-21. Tékna refers to those who were born of God
and huioí refers to those who show maturity acting
as sons. When just the basic relationship as the born
again child of God is referred to, it is expressed as
tékna (Rom.8:16). Huiós gives evidence of the dignity
of one's relationship with the Father or the expression
of His character.[11]

With regards to that, when the expression "children of God"
is used, it refers to those who have received Christ and are
born of God or regenerated in their human spirit. We have
the inner witnessing in our spirit to the fact that we are the
children of God. The Indwelling Spirit also witnesses to this

most basic and elementary relationship with God (Rom.8:16).

Whereas the Spirit testifies with our spirit that we are God's children (Rom.8:16), only those who are led by the Spirit are sons of God (Rom.8:14). Here lies the twofold foundational work of the indwelling Spirit: He brings forth the children of God and testifies of the divine birth, and He leads them into maturity to be the sons of God. We are regenerated as the children of God in order that we might be led to grow into maturity as the sons of God. In short, a child of God is divinely birthed, but a son of God is divinely led.

The Greek word for *lead* is *ago*. It has several biblical usages, which include:-
  • to take by laying hold of, and in this way to bring to the point of destination
  • to lead by accompanying one to (into) a place
  • to lead, guide, direct, rule, govern, control

The same word *ago* was used when the disciples *brought* (Greek: *ago*) the colt to Jesus to sit on it (Mt.21:7; Lk. 19:35; Mk. 11:7). A rope was tied around the neck of the animal and pulled by a string. The colt could not do what she wanted. In the same way, the sons of God are those who are led, driven and controlled by the Spirit so that they could not do as they pleased. A believer can be a child of God without being led, driven and controlled by the Spirit, for unless he gives up control, the Spirit cannot take full control of him.

It is significant to note that the colt was not brought to a place of her choosing, rather, she was brought to Jesus to become a vessel of honor to be ridden by the King of kings to enter the city of peace, Jerusalem, for the accomplishment of God's purpose. God's intention and heart's desire is to lead us by the Indwelling Spirit in order to bring us to a point of destination to become sons of God where we might become the vessel of honor for the fulfillment of His eternal purpose. Without the leading of the Spirit, we will never fulfill the plan of God for our lives i.e. to become His matured sons.

Instead of being led by the Spirit, believers are often driven and controlled by their own personal needs, wants and longings and would often ask God to serve their personal interests. Many believers lack the crucial understanding that the ministry of the Indwelling Spirit is to bring forth matured sons that can take their God's given responsibility and not to produce infantile believers that are only preoccupied with the ideas of God bringing them to a destination of personal success in life and a place of self-gratification. The Spirit does indeed meet our personal needs but He does so for a divine purpose of bringing the believers into full sonship. According to Romans 8:14, the sons of God are led, driven and controlled by the Spirit to reach a point of destination (the point of conforming to the image of Christ) and to come to a place of maturity (the place of sonship). To be the sons of God, our daily living and walking must be consistently led, guided, directed, ruled, driven, controlled and governed by the Spirit so that we might be the same as Christ is, in life and nature, in words and deeds, in expression and constitution. It is for this reason that Romans 8:15 designated the Spirit as the Spirit of sonship[12] as the sons of God are produced by the Spirit's inward operation in leading the believers to grow and mature in the divine life unto full sonship.

Like Paul, Apostle John also conveyed a clear understanding regarding the necessity of believers to be in the process of growth in life in order to reach maturity to be the sons of God. He sees the believers as students of the Earth School, who must start as "babies in Christ", progressing to become "young men" and ultimately maturing as "fathers". The "babies in Christ" are believers who have just received the divine life, the "young men" are those who are growing in the divine life and the "fathers" are those who are matured in the divine life.

> *1 John 2:12-14 NIV*
> *I write to you, dear children (Greek: teknion), because your sins have been forgiven on account of his name. I write to you, fathers, because you have known him who is from the beginning. I write to you, young men, because you have overcome the evil one. I write to you, dear children (Greek: paidion), because you have known the Father. I write to you, fathers, because you have known him who is from the beginning. I write to you, young men, because you are strong, and the word of God lives in you, and you have overcome the evil one.*

John addressed all believers as "children", *teknion*, on the basis that their sins are forgiven when they believe in Christ. By receiving Christ as life, the believers are born of Him to become the children of God (John 1:12-13). However, as "children"(*teknion*) all believers do not have the same standing and stature, and they are classified according to the different degrees of growth in the divine life.

The lowest station of the Earth School is the babies in Christ or *paidion*. These are the ones who have just received the divine life and have the experiential knowledge of God as their begetting Father. These babies or infants in Christ have an intimate relationship with the Father and have received the Spirit of sonship by which they cry out "Abba! Father!" (Rom.8:15). However, being still in the stage of spiritual infancy, they are deficient in spiritual understanding. Some believers in the church of Corinth were in this category. To them, Paul gave this instruction, "Brethren, do not be children (*paidion*) in your thinking (1 Co.14:20)." These believers were children in their thinking, reasoning and understanding because of the lack of growth in the divine life.

As the believers continue to pursue the growth of divine life, they progress to attain to the next level of the Earth School and become the "young men" of God. These "young men" are the strong believers that have overcome the evil one, for the word of God dwells in them richly, thus energizing, empowering, strengthening, nourishing and sustaining them. Through the nourishment from the abiding word of God, the believers grow up in the divine life and become "young men".

The highest station of the Earth School consists of the "fathers". These are the ones that have "known Him who is from the beginning". In John's words, the One who is from the beginning was Christ Himself (John 1:1; 1 John 1:1). This means that the "fathers" are believers that have reached the maturity of divine life, for they have the full knowledge and experience of Christ. The "fathers" are believers who are constantly conforming to the image of Christ the Firstborn, and groaning inwardly, eagerly awaiting their sonship which is the redemption of the body (Rom.8:29; 23). Both the Apostles Paul and John are considered the "fathers", for they were willing to relinquish everything in order to gain Christ. Paul expressed his earnest desire to be continually transformed in order to be made conformable to Christ's death in the hope that he might achieve the goal of sonship i.e. the glorification of the body. He said emphatically in Philippians 3:10-11, "that I may know Him and the power of His resurrection and the fellowship of His sufferings, being conformed to His death; in order that I may attain to the resurrection from the dead"(NASB).

John also expressed his earnest expectation for the return of the Lord in order to obtain the full sonship, the glorification of the body. He told the believers, "Beloved, now we are the children (Greek: *teknon*) of God, and it has not appeared as yet what we will be. We know that when He appears, we will be like Him, because we will see Him just as He is. And everyone who has this hope fixed on Him purifies himself, just as He is pure" (1 John 3:2-3 NASB).

Both Paul and John anticipated the completion of sonship that will occur when the Lord returns to redeem our bodies. That will be the time when there will be a public revelation of the manifested sons of God and believers will share in the resurrection of the Firstborn Son of God. Therefore, to grow in maturity to be the sons of God, we must see sonship through a spirit of revelation and devote ourselves to the teachings of the apostles so that we would diligently undergo the process of divine birth, growth and maturation in order to obtain full sonship. We must also reject the erroneous concept that "children of God" and "sons of God" are synonymous, as this would hinder us from having a proper understanding concerning the significance of sonship in God's purpose.

Adoption versus Sonship

A clear understanding of sonship according to the divine revelation is essential for us to participate in what God had foreordained and prepared for His children. Since sonship is the very purpose of God even before the foundation of the world, our understanding concerning sonship must match God's thinking and God's heart's desire. Regrettably, just as many Bible translations not only failed to make an appropriate distinction between "children" and "sons", they also incorrectly translated the Greek word *huiothesia* as "adoption" or "adoption as sons" rather than rightly translate it as "sonship" (Rom.8:15, 23; 9:4; Gal.4: 5; Eph.1: 5).[13]

Kenneth S. Wuest has made a helpful analysis of the word *huiothesia* in his comments on Ephesians 1:5:-

> The Greek word is huiothesia, from tithemi, "to place", and huios, "an adult son." Thus, the word refers to the act of God placing these selected-out ones as adult sons. Paul speaks of this in Romans 8:15 in the words 'Spirit of adoption." The apostle here uses as an illustration the Roman practice of legally adopting a child, and thus not only bequeathing to him the material possessions of the one adopting, but also giving him his civil status. Thus God takes a believing sinner, regenerates him, and by means of this makes him His child (teknon, a born one). Then He takes this child and places him in a legal position as an adult son (huios). We thus become joint-heirs with Christ, having been raised to a civil status as adult sons, in which we become heirs of God, inheriting jointly with Christ all that He possesses as an heir of God the Father by virtue of His Sonship and work on the Cross. This is one object of God's predestination. The other

> is that the believer is to be conformed to the image
> of God's Son (Rom.8:29). Thus, God selected certain
> from among mankind to be included within the saving
> work of Christ, and those selected, He predestined to
> be placed as adult sons and to be conformed to the
> image of His own son....He previously marked us out
> with a view to placing us as adult sons for Himself,
> for His own satisfaction, that He might be glorified in
> saving us and being the recipient of our worship and
> service.[14]

Wuest's word study helps us to understand that God's way of placing His selected ones into sonship is by means of a judicial procedure of legally adopting us and giving us the civil status as adult sons to become the joint heirs of Christ. In Paul's time, adoption was a legal act by which a person enters another family and comes under the authority of the father of the new family. Adoption of adult men was a convenient recourse for childless couple or individual, and particularly for emperors in need of successors. Through the legal act of adoption, the adoptee's old relationship was severed and his old debts and obligations cancelled. The adopted son has the same right to inheritance as the natural son. Judicially, the same meaning applies to every child of God. We no longer owe any allegiance to our old masters as we now owe total allegiance to God the Father. As members of His household, we are placed in the legal position as adult sons and are qualified to inherit every benefit belonging to God's heirs.

However, this notion of the judicial procedure of adoption is insufficient and incomplete to convey the true and biblical meaning of sonship as God has intended. Sonship does not merely involve the judicial act of justification. It also includes a divine organic process of birth and growth to fullness of maturity. God does not merely justifying us judicially but also regenerating us organically with His divine life. God is truly our begetting Father and we are the true partakers of His divine life and nature. Sonship, then, is an organic reality based on divine life and not merely a legal pronouncement or a judicial act.

Since adoption is the deliberate act of a person, or an individual, to accept someone not natural to him as his legal child or son, the inappropriate use of the word *adoption* in bible translations would imply that a believer enters into relationship with God merely by God's legal act of adoption. This is far from the truth for every child of God. In the case of civil adoption, the adopted child does not bear any biological resemblance and characteristics of the adopted parents. Thus, while civil adoption can give someone a legal position and status of a son, it could never give the child the nature of the father. However, according to the divine revelation, we are called children of God simply because we are actually born of God and are God's children per se and not due to any legal act of adoption. Sonship must thus be understood in the context that God genuinely begets us by divine birth and we are indeed His very real, actual, genuine children —possessors of His very life and partakers of His own nature (Jn. 1:13; 3:6; Rom. 8:16; 1 Jn. 2:29;3:9;4:7;5:1,4,18; 2 Pe.1:4).

With the divine birth as the beginning, God's children must then continue with the organic process of divine growth into maturity in order to conform to the image of Christ the Firstborn. This divine growth into maturity is again not a judicial procedure but an organic process. Just as a human being cannot become a child of God without the divine birth, so a child of God cannot become a son of God without the divine growth. Thus, the biblical concept of sonship involves both the organic processes of divine birth and divine growth.

To be lacking this crucial understanding of sonship and to merely regard sonship as the judicial procedure of adoption is to fall short of the divine revelation that matches God's purpose and satisfies God's heart's desire, and to deny God's ability to beget us with His divine life and to reproduce us to become the duplication of Christ, the prototype of the many sons to follow.

It is by the organic processes of divine birth and growth that we can become matured in the divine life and hence qualify for sonship. Sonship is thus an organic process which ends with a qualification. Sonship begins with the divine birth and must continue with divine growth to reach divine maturity. Sonship is brought into completion by our full conformity to the image of Christ (to be the same as He is in life and nature) and likeness of Christ (by our bodily transfiguration on the Lord's return). This attainment of sonship thus qualifies us to become the co-heirs with Christ. According to Romans 8:17, to qualify as the heirs of God and joint heirs with Christ, we must suffer with Christ (taking after Christ as our example of maturity into sonship) so that we may also be glorified with Him (sharing in the power of His bodily resurrection when He returns). Glorification is a qualification —it is not a legal right for every believer. It must be earned by taking after Christ as our pattern of suffering and our model of perfection and maturity. It is by glorification that will qualify us as heirs of God and joint-heirs with Christ.

The word "heir", *kleronomos*, is closely linked to the concept of sonship. Galatians 4:7b says, "...since you are a son, God has made you also an heir." Likewise, Revelations 21:7 says, "He who overcomes shall inherit all things, and I will be his God and he shall be My son." An heir is one who receives his allotted possession by right of sonship. (A coheir or a joint-heir is one who obtains something assigned to himself together with others i.e. one who participates in the same lot). Thus, both the words "heir" and "son" indicate maturity. The attainment of our divine adulthood as the sons of God will qualify us to be heirs of God. In ancient times, it was a requirement for a child to come into full age as a son before he could inherit the portion allotted to him. This understanding was clearly brought up by the apostle Paul, who indicated that a child is only a potential heir but not necessarily a real heir, for a child in his position and status is in actual fact no different from the standing of a slave:-

> *Galatians 4:1-7 NIV*
> *What I am saying is that as long as the heir is a child, he is no different from a slave, although he owns the whole estate. He is subject to guardians and trustees until the time set by his father. So also, when we were children, we were in slavery under the basic principles of the world. But when the time had fully come, God sent his Son, born of a woman, born under law, to redeem those under law, that we might receive the full rights of sons. Because you are sons, God sent the Spirit of his Son into our hearts, the Spirit who calls out, "Abba, Father." So you are no longer a slave, but a son; and since you are a son, God has made you also an heir.*

To summarize, sonship, being the centre of the divine purpose, is to ultimately gain human beings as God's sons to be the full heirs of God and joint heirs with Christ. In order for us to be conferred with a new status as God's heir to inherit all that God is and has for us, we must undergo three progressive stages: (1) **born of God as His children**; (2) **grow into maturity as God's sons**; (3) **be legalized and qualified as God's heirs**. We see the reflection of these divine truths in the ancient story told in the beginning: the prince became the heir of the father's kingdom by undergoing the natural processes of birth, growth and maturity. The conferring of his kingship and the legalization of his heirship took place only when the prince has passed all the necessary trials and tests to bring him into a place of full maturity. In the like manner, believers as the children of God must pass all the tests and sufferings in the Earth School to grow into maturity as God's sons in order that they might be legalized and qualified as the heirs of God and joint-heirs with Christ to participate in the ruling and reigning of the earth in the Millennium kingdom, and ultimately, to be possessors of the New Jerusalem and inheritors of the New Heaven and New Earth in the eternity future.

A CHILD   A SON   AN HEIR

The Three Stages of Sonship

Putting Away Childish Things

To respond heartily to God's call to sonship and to attain maturity of life, we must first be willing to put away all childish things, which is to put behind all our childish thinking and childish speaking. Paul, in his letter to the Corinthians' believers, extorted them to put all the childish ways aside in order that they might develop maturity of character to possess the virtues of faith, hope and love, thus taking upon themselves the manifested qualities of Christ's own nature.

> *1 Corinthians 13:11-12 NIV*
> *When I was a child, I talked like a child, I thought like a child, I reasoned like a child. When I became a man, I put childish ways behind me. Now we see but a poor reflection as in a mirror; then we shall see face to face. Now I know in part; then I shall know fully, even as I am fully known.*

Here, Paul likened a person who lacks the maturity of character to a child. The Greek word for child here is *nepios*, from *ne* (not) and *epo* (to speak). It refers to one who is not yet speaking or unable to speak fluently. This word is used to describe an infant or baby in Christ, a person weak in faith, a beginner or simply someone that has not grown up. These are the believers who are not only dull in hearing but also unskilled and not experienced in the word of righteousness.

> *Hebrew 5:11-14; 6:1 NIV*
> *We have much to say about this, but it is hard to explain because you are slow to learn. In fact, though by this time you ought to be teachers, you need someone to teach you the elementary truths of God's word all over*

again. You need milk, not solid food! Anyone who lives
on milk, being still an infant (Greek: nepios), is not
acquainted with the teaching about righteousness.
But solid food is for the mature, who by constant use
have trained themselves to distinguish good from evil.
Therefore let us leave the elementary teachings about
Christ and go on to maturity.

Not forsaking childish ways would mean that we would
remain in spiritual infancy, and thus unable to understand
and comprehend the crucial element of sonship in God's
purpose. Without divine growth into maturity, we will be
childish in our thinking and unable to speak creative words
of life and faith in love. The book of Ephesians describes
immature believers as children that are forever changing
their minds, for they are easily tossed to and fro like ships by
waves and blown here and there by every wind of deceitful
teachings, doctrines, concepts and opinions. To attain
maturity of character, believers must speak the truth in love
to each other in order to grow in the divine life.

> *Ephesians: 14-16 NIV*
> *Then we will no longer be infants (Greek: nepios),*
> *tossed back and forth by the waves, and blown here*
> *and there by every wind of teaching and by the cunning*
> *and craftiness of men in their deceitful scheming.*
> *Instead, speaking the truth in love, we will in all things*
> *grow up into him who is the Head, that is, Christ. From*
> *him the whole body, joined and held together by every*
> *supporting ligament, grows and builds itself up in love,*
> *as each part does its work.*

If believers fail to put away childish things and continually
neglect the divine call to full sonship, there is a great danger
that believers will be failing in the following crucial aspects:-

- Failing to satisfy the Father's heart's desire and thus failing to fulfill His eternal purpose;
- Failing to appropriate the full provision of the cross accomplished by the all inclusive death of Christ and thus failing to walk in full victory and complete liberty that is found in Christ;
- Failing to fully co-operate with the Spirit for growth in the divine life and thus failing to conform to the image of Christ the Firstborn;
- Failing to nurture and build up the regenerated spirit to grow in spiritual strength and thus failing to overcome the self, the flesh, the world and Satan;
- Failing to be a functional and effective member of the Body of Christ and thus failing in the building up of the Church unto fullness of maturity to be presented to Christ as a glorious Church — holy and blameless;
- Failing to receive the full inheritance of sonship and the kingdom rewards and thus failing to become joint heirs of God and co-kings with Christ to rule in the millennium kingdom;
- Failing to build on "gold, silver and precious stones"(1 Co.3:12) and thus failing to be incorporated as the New Jerusalem to be the ultimate expression of God's glory throughout eternity.

The Mingling Cry of the Spirit with our spirit: Abba, Father

How do we progress from being the children of God to become sons of God conforming to the image of Christ the Firstborn? The key is the Indwelling Spirit with our spirit. The Indwelling Spirit is the Spirit of sonship, for His inward operation is for the purpose of producing the many sons of God (Rom.8:15). The Spirit first enters into our spirit to initiate the birthing of our spirit through regeneration to make us His children. He then indwells and mingles with our spirit to fill and energize our spirit with newness of life and power. The regenerated spirit mingled with God's Spirit becomes the channel and means to transmit the divine life into the soul to constitute us as the sons of God. By this spreading of the Spirit from our spirit to saturate and permeate the soul with the divine life, our soul will be conformed to the image of Christ through the process of transformation from glory to glory. This organic work of the Spirit will ultimately conclude with the transfiguration of the body at the Lord's return, thus bringing our sonship into completion and consummation.[15]

From the moment we are born of the Spirit to become the children of God, there is a deep longing within us to grow and mature in the divine life so that we might conform to the image of God's Son and become manifested sons of God on the Lord's return. We groan inwardly in our spirit as we wait for the redemption of our body — our manifestation as God's sons. The Spirit also comes to our aid and bears us up in our weakness by interceding for us with unspeakable yearnings or groanings too deep for utterance:-

Romans 8: 23, 26 NASB
...even we ourselves groan within ourselves, waiting
eagerly for our adoption as sons, the redemption of
our body....In the same way the Spirit also helps our
weakness; for we do not know how to pray as we
should, but the Spirit Himself intercedes for us with
groanings too deep for words.

Here we see the joint-groaning of our spirit with God's Spirit. The groaning of our spirit is our inner witness, proving that we are genuinely God's children by the divine birth. Such an inward groaning also expresses our earnest desire to conform to the image of Christ and to be free from all childish things which lock us up in our spiritual infantilism. The Spirit groans in our groaning to intercede for us so that we might experience His transforming work to bring us into maturity as sons of God.

The spirit of sonship is a travailing spirit. We groan and travail in our spirit, aided by the Spirit, in the hope that we will be liberated from the slavery of corruption and brought into the glorious freedom of the children of God (Rom.8:21). This liberation is primarily for our setting free or deliverance from the self (the corrupted soul life), the flesh (the body of sin), the world and Satan in order for us to be an overcomer and a grown up son of God. Paul also spoke of this groaning or travailing as the mingling cry of the Spirit with our spirit to call upon God as "Abba, Father."

Romans 8:15 RSV
For you did not receive the spirit of slavery to fall back
into fear, but you have received the spirit of sonship.
When we cry, "Abba! Father!"

Galatians 4:6 RSV
And because you are sons, God has sent the Spirit of

> *his Son into our hearts, crying, "Abba! Father!"*

The Greek word for "cry" is *krazo*; it speaks of expressing a deep emotion with a loud cry or vociferation. Note that in Romans 8:15, it is our spirit that cries out "Abba, Father", and in Galatians 4:6, it is the Spirit that cries out "Abba, Father". Further studies of these two words reveal meaningful insights concerning the role of the mingled spirit (the Holy Spirit with our spirit) in achieving the goal of sonship.

Abba is an Aramaic word for "Papa", a term of great intimacy between a father and a child. It is normally the first word a child would utter in recognition of his father. The Aramaic language was a late Persian dialect of the Assyrian language and had become the standard language of Jewish politics and religion after the intertestamental period. Most Jews in Palestine at the time of Jesus spoke Aramaic as one of their native tongues. However, such a term *Abba* was never addressed to God directly in prayer. Hence, a mingling cry "Abba" signifies the bearing of joint testimony and witnessing of the Spirit with our spirit in our relationship with God —that we are children of God, being born of God, by the Spirit.

"Father" is the translation from the Greek word *pater*. Only a child in a more advanced stage of growth into adulthood would be more familiar to use this term. The conquests of Alexander the Great took the Greek language everywhere, and Greek became the language of the world from 300 B.C. to A.D.300.[16] While a Jew might speak Hebrew and Aramaic in their private and domestic life, they spoke Greek in their business, commercial and public lives. A grown up child would be accustomed to the Greek language so that he might be more privileged and have an advantage with commercial dealings in the Greek-speaking world or to be better equipped to continue his father's business.

Notwithstanding this, the Greek term *pater* for father was hardly even used by the Jews in their religious practices and in their prayers to God, as they would normally address God as Jehovah or Adonai. The mingling cry of our spirit with the Spirit to call upon God as "Father" thus speaks of a higher level of relationship between God and the grown up believers. It refers to those who show maturity and responsibility by acting as grown up sons.

During Jesus' earthly ministry, He went against the traditional and conventional way by specifically addressing God as 'Abba" or "Papa" to introduce the special and affectionate relationship between a regenerated believer and God the Father. Moreover, the Lord Jesus used the Greek title, "Pater" to describe His affectionate relationship with the Father as a real Son that expressed and represented the Father's character. At the age of twelve, He was already aware of His relationship to God the Father. Replying to His anxious mother who had searched for Him for three days and had finally found him in the temple court sitting among the teachers, Jesus said, "Why did you seek Me? Did you not know that I must be about My Father's business?" (Lk.2:49). Again, from the outset of His ministry at thirty, He cleansed the temple by driving out the merchants with words of rebuke, "Get these out of here! How dare you turn my Father's house into a market", thus publicly expressed His zeal of minding His Father's business (Jn.2:13-17). The final word before His last breath at the cross was a loud cry, "Father, into your hands I commit my spirit" (Lk. 23:46) which became the strongest evidence of His maturity in acting as God's Son and completing the work which the Father has given Him to do (Jn.17:4).

Thus, *Abba* is used by the Lord to show His intimate and especially close relationship with His Father. *Pater* is used by the Lord to show His obedience as God's matured Son; to the point that He was willing to humbly submit Himself to do the Father's will by laying down His life to suffer in the hands of sinful men and taking the sin of mankind upon Himself. Jesus issued forth a prayer in the garden of Gethsemane by crying out to God as "Abba Father". Thus, He showed us that we too, must not only have an intimate relationship with the Father as God's children, but also demonstrate the Father's nature, character and attributes as God's matured sons — ones that know how to take responsibility in caring for the Father's business in full obedience to His will and total commitment to His work.

> *Mark 14:32-36 NIV*
> *They went to a place called Gethsemane, and Jesus said to his disciples, "Sit here while I pray." He took Peter, James and John along with him, and he began to be deeply distressed and troubled. "My soul is overwhelmed with sorrow to the point of death," he said to them. "Stay here and keep watch." Going a little farther, he fell to the ground and prayed that if possible the hour might pass from him "Abba, Father,"* *he said, "everything is possible for you. Take this cup from me. Yet not what I will, but what you will."*

> *Hebrews 5:7-10 NIV*
> *During the days of Jesus' life on earth, he offered up prayers and petitions with loud cries and tears to the one who could save him from death, and he was heard because of his reverent submission. Although he was a son, he learned obedience from what he suffered and, once made perfect, he became the source of eternal salvation for all who obey him and was designated by God to be high priest in the order of Melchizedek.*

As we are led by the Holy Spirit day by day, there will be an increase or intensification of the mingling cry of our spirit with the Spirit in anticipation of the coming manifestation of the sons of God. There is even now an intense deep cry of the mingled spirit inside every child of God to urge each of us to press on towards growth and maturity in the divine life so that we might be progressively transformed to conform to the image of Christ the Firstborn. This continuous mingling cry of our spirit with the Spirit is our most sweet and precious prayers to our Father, and the final hour has almost come for Him to answer our deep mingling cry. Soon, the Father will send forth His firstborn Son to receive us as the Bride and to bring His many sons into glory — and when He comes, He will change our lowly bodies into glorious bodies like His own.

All believers in Christ must now heed the earnest invitation of the Spirit and the Bride to participate in God's call to divine sonship. The last chapter of the book of Revelations urges us with this very clear message, "The Spirit and the bride say, "Come!"" (Rev.22:17).

Will we heed the Father's call to divine sonship? If this is the deep cry of your spirit and the earnest desire of your heart, let's respond to the Father's call by coming before Him in prayer:

> *Father, I thank you that you have predestined me unto sonship. You have chosen me in Christ even before the foundation of the world to be your son. I thank you that Jesus is the firstborn of the many sons of God and He is the one that I must conform to as my prototype and model for sonship. Father, I thank you that through divine birth, I have become your child. And as your child, I share in your divine life and nature. My spirit bears witness that I am your child. O, you are my Abba, Father. You are my*

Papa, my Daddy. O, Abba Father, I cry out to you, let me be yours and yours only. I am now heeding your call, to grow up into maturity to become your son. Father, I am confident of this, that you have begun a good work in me and will carry it onto completion until the day of Christ Jesus. Father, sanctify me through and through so that my whole spirit, soul and body will be kept blameless until the coming of the Lord Jesus Christ. I believe that You, the one who has called me, is faithful and will surely accomplish your divine plan and purpose in my life. I commit my life to you.

In Jesus' name, Amen.

Notes I

1. Paul E.Billheimer, *Destined For The Throne* (Christian Literature Crusade, 1975), pp37-38.
2. Kenneth S.Wuest., *The New Testament : An Expanded Translation* (Wm.B.Eerdmans Publishing Co.1961), p 449
3. Joseph Bryant Rotherham, *The Emphasized Bible* (Kregel Publications, 1994), New Testament p196
4. Spiros Zodhiates, *The Complete Word Study New Testament – Lexical Aids to the New Testament* (World Bible Publishers, 1991), Strong #1586, p910
5. Genesis 6:2 was a controversial text but Jude 6-7 gives favor that it refers to the fallen angels.
6. In the following scriptures, King David can be seen as a type of the Lord Jesus Christ, the King of the millennium: Jer.30:9, Eze.34:23, 37:24; Hos.3:5. Solomon also typified Christ as the seed of David, the One who builds the real temple of God (the Church) and inherits the throne and kingdom of David (2 Sam.7:12-13; Luke 1:32-33).
7. Positionally, the saved believers are sons of God and this right to sonship can only be brought to full realization when they progress into maturity in the divine growth. The manifested sons of God must be redeemed, regenerated, transformed and glorified. All believers are invited to fully participate in God's organic salvation so that they might grow in the divine life to mature as sons of God. See also note 9.
8. So sacred is this special Name peculiar to God that that it was said that the Jews did not utter it on ordinary occasions as it was only to be pronounced by the High Priest on the Day of Atonement.
9. The born again believers are called sons of God only in reference to the initial stage of sonship or the stage of regeneration of the human spirit (Gal.3:26; 4:6-7). We will refer to believers in this initial stage of sonship as children of God. The term "sons of God" is reserved for believers who have undergone a more advanced stage of growth in the divine life until they attain full maturity in the divine life (evidenced by the transformation of the soul and ultimately, the glorification of the body).
10. For instance, the Authorized King James Version had erroneously translated the Greek word *tékna* as "sons" rather than "children". Perhaps realizing this inaccuracy and lack of clear distinction between children and sons in the Authorized King James Version, the New King James Version conveys a more accurate distinction between the two. This is noticeable in the following verses:-

   Ephesians 1:5
   "Having predestined us unto adoption of children by Jesus Christ to himself, according to the good pleasure of his will (KJV)." "Having predestined us to adoption as sons by Jesus Christ to Himself, according to the good pleasure of his will (NKJV)."

   John 1:12
   "But as many as received him, to them gave he power to become the sons of God, even to them that believe on his name (KJV)." "But as many as received Him, to them He gave the right to become children of God, to those who believe in His name (NKJV)."

   1 John 3:1-2
   "Behold, what manner of love the Father hath bestowed upon us, that we should be called the sons of God.....Beloved, now are we the sons

of God, and it doth not yet appear what we shall be: but we know that,
when he shall appear, we shall be like him; for we shall see him as he
is (KJV)." "Behold what manner of love the Father has bestowed on
us, that we should be called children of God!......Beloved, now we are
children of God; and it has not yet been revealed what we shall be, but
we know that when He is revealed, we shall be like Him, for we shall see
Him as He is (NKJV)."

Perhaps motivated by a desire for gender equality, Today's New International Version
(TNIV), on the other hand, translated all New Testament verses on "sons" (huiós) as
"children" (Mat.5:9;44-45, Luke 6:35;20:36; John 12:36; Rom.8:14,19,9:26,3:7,26;
Gal.4:6-7, 1 Thel 5:5, Rev.21:7). For Hebrews 2:10, TNIV has translated "in bringing
many sons to glory" as "in bringing many sons and daughters to glory", keeping sons
and inserting daughters. Such tampering with the Word of God, either by changing it
or adding to it, is a matter of extreme seriousness.

11. Spiros Zodhiates, The Complete Word Study New Testament – Lexical Aids to the
New Testament (World Bible Publishers, 1991), Strong #5207, p962.
12. The Greek word pneuma can refer to either God's Spirit or the human spirit. NIV
translates Romans 8:15 as "you received the Spirit of sonship". Amplified Bible
speaks of "the Spirit producing sonship". RSV translates it as "you have received the
spirit of sonship." "Spirit of sonship" and "spirit of sonship" are acceptable
translations, for the Spirit mingles with our own spirit to become one spirit.
13. For instance, only the NIV, RSV and Jerusalem Bible have rightly translated huiothesia
in Romans 8:15 as "sonship", but most other translations render this word as
"adoption".
14. Kenneth S.Wuest., Word Studies from Greek New Testament, Vol.1, (Wm.B.Eerdmans
Publishing Co.1961), pp 36-37.
15. This transforming and consummating work of the Spirit to produce sons has an
outward sign which gives evidence that the manifestation of the sons of God is at
hand. The outward sign is the groaning of the whole creation, waiting eagerly for
the revealing of the sons of God (Rom.8:19-22). The groaning of the whole creation
is neither symbolic nor metaphorical. The creation has life of its own. Every plant,
each animal, every bit of the creation, all mountains, forests, seas, winds and
thing on earth has intelligence, desire and will within it (Amos 1:2; Ps 98:8; Lk 19:40)
The creation was given by God to man to take dominion over, to keep and to guard
(Gen.1;26,28;2:15). However, as a result of man's fall, the creation was cursed and
is at present enslaved under the law of decay and corruption (Gen.3:17; Ro.8:21).

In addition, man lost dominion over the creation which was gained by Satan, who
is now the god of this world (Mt.4:8-9; 2 Co.4:4). Satanic and demonic abuses of
the creation have subjected the creation to further frustration and futility. The creation
is now anxiously longing for the manifestation of the sons of God so that it may be
free from the slavery of corruption and bondage of decay. The groaning of the whole
creation is noticeable by the increase in frequency and intensity of natural disasters
such as tsunami, earthquakes, volcanic eruptions, hurricanes, floods, etc in our days.
These physical manifestations signify that the Lord's return is near to rapture the
Church and to consummate the Spirit's work to produce the many sons of God. The
Lord's coming back will usher in the 1000 years' rule upon the earth by the sons of
God to set the creation free from decay and corruption.
16. Greek was the most commonly used language in everyday commerce and was widely
understood throughout the Roman Empire. Koine Greek was unofficially the first or
second language in the Roman Empire.

Part 2

The Divine Dispensation

Part 2

The Divine Dispensation

The Family and Household of God

In *The Call to Sonship*, we explored the significance of sonship in God's purpose — God's good pleasure and heart's desire is to gain many sons to become the members of His household. One of God's divine titles revealed in the Bible is "Father". The apostle Paul prayed in Ephesians 3:14-15, "For this reason I bow my knees before the Father, from whom every family in heaven and on earth derives its name" (NASB). In the Bible, *father* is a term used to denote 'source' and 'origin'. In a broader sense, God is the source and origin of all the human families on earth and the angelic family in heaven (even though angels are neither married nor given in marriage, they derived their origin from God and are thus called the sons of God in Job 1:6). Therefore, God is called 'Father' of all rational and intelligent beings, whether men or angels because He is their source, originator, creator, preserver, guardian and protector. Hebrew 12:9 says that God is the Father of spirits, thus indicates that all spirit beings (be it angels or men) derive their existence and origin from God.

However, the genuine usage of the word *father* must also connote the idea of birth. This means that God can only be the Father of those who are begotten of Him in their spirits. He is the Father of the spirits of the regenerated human beings, a genuine Father to those who are of the household of faith (Gal.6:10).The Greek word for *family* is *patria*, derived from *pater*, which means "of the linkage, belongs to or spring from a father". In extension, the Greek word for *household* is *oikeios*, derived from *oikos* (a house or household) which carries the meaning "a person belonging to a certain household". For instance, Joseph was said to be of the house and family of David (Lk.2:4) which means that Joseph was of the lineage of David and an extension of David's household through blood relationship. Strictly speaking, no family or household can exist without being related in blood. Likewise, it is through the blood of Christ (His life-releasing death) that we are spiritually related and connected to God, becoming His household and His family. His blood not only redeems us from sins but also gives us life. Ephesians 2:18-19 says, "for through Him we both have our access in one Spirit to the Father. So then you are no longer strangers and aliens, but you are fellow citizens with the saints, and are of God's household" (NASB). Who are we as believers in Christ? We are the members of God's household. We are the family of God. We are the lineage of God, the extension of God and the enlargement of God!

God's intention to raise a family and a household on earth with many divine sons genuinely begotten of Him is marvelously shadowed in the Old Testament types. One of such type can be seen in the changing of Abraham's name from Abram (which means *exalted father*) to Abraham (which means *father of a multitude*) (Gen.17:5). In typology, Abram typifies God as the Father of Creation and Abraham typifies God as the Father of Regeneration or a begetting Father. For the satisfaction of His heart's desire and the fulfillment of His eternal purpose, God must be the Father that begets children from all nations, tribes, peoples and tongues (Rev.7:9) and not just a Creator and an exalted Father who brought into existence all the families of God's creatures. The believers are the genuine family of God and of God's household not because they are God's created creatures but because they are God's regenerated children. The believers' crying out and calling to God as "Abba, Father" from deep within their spirit testifies and confirms that they are born of God (Rom.8:15). It is the divine birth and not the natural birth that qualifies the believers to become the children of God (Jn.1:12-13).

God's purpose is ultimately related to the gaining of His many sons to become His family and His household. How does God carry out and accomplish this grand purpose? Since God's PURPOSE is the divine sonship, we shall now examine the MEANS by which God carries out and accomplishes His eternal purpose. This MEANS is **the Divine Dispensation** which includes a divine plan, a divine arrangement and a divine administration by which God carries out the divine dispensing of the divine life for the attainment of the goal of sonship.

God's Household's Plan, Arrangement and Administration

After introducing the crucial concept of divine sonship as God's PURPOSE, Paul continues in the Book of Ephesians to unfold the pertinent and foundational truth of the Divine Dispensation as God's MEANS for the accomplishment of His eternal purpose.

> *Ephesians 1:9-14 KJV*
> *Having made known unto us the mystery of his will, according to his good pleasure which he hath purposed in himself: That in the **dispensation** of the fullness of times he might gather together in one all things in Christ, both which are in heaven, and which are on earth, even in him: In whom also we have obtained an inheritance, being predestinated according to the purpose of him who worketh all things after the counsel of his own will: That we should be to the praise of his glory, who first trusted in Christ. In whom ye also trusted, after that ye heard the word of truth, the gospel of your salvation: in whom also after that ye believed, ye were sealed with that Holy Spirit of promise, which is the earnest of our inheritance until the redemption of the purchase possession, unto the praise of his glory. (emphasis mine)*

We now know that sonship is the goal of God's eternal purpose and we have briefly introduced the term *Divine Dispensation* as the means that God uses for the accomplishment of this purpose. What then is the Divine Dispensation? Let us look at two other scriptural references where the crucial word dispensation is used:

Ephesians 3:1-6 KJV
For this cause I Paul, the prisoner of Jesus Christ for you Gentiles, if ye have heard of the **dispensation of the grace of God** *which is given me to you-ward: How that by revelation he made known unto me a mystery; (as I wrote afore in few words, whereby, when ye read, ye may understand my knowledge in the mystery of Christ) which in other ages was not made known unto the sons of men, as it is now revealed unto his holy apostles and prophets by the Spirit; that the Gentiles should be fellow heirs, and of the same body, and partakers of the promise in Christ by the gospel. (emphasis mine)*

Colossians 1:25-27 KJV
Whereof I am made a minister, according to the **dispensation of God** *which is given to me for you, to fulfill the word of God; even the mystery which hath been hid from ages and from generations, but now is made manifest to his saints: to whom God would make known what is the riches of the glory of this mystery among the Gentiles; which is Christ in you, the hope of glory. (emphasis mine)*

The word *dispensation* comes from the Greek word *oikonomai*[1] (from *oikos*, "a house" and *nomos*, "a law"). **The central idea of dispensation is that of managing or administrating of the affairs in a household**. God not only desires a household, but also purposed in Himself the means to manage and administrate the affairs of His household. Easton's Bible Dictionary defines *dispensation* as "the method or scheme according to which God carries out his purposes toward men".[2] According to the American Heritage® Dictionary, *dispensation* is "a specific arrangement or system by which something is dispensed".[3]

In the eternity past, God has a secret ambition, a heart's

desire. It is to bring forth many sons to become members of His Household. To accomplish this mysterious plan and purpose, God has made an arrangement and designed an administrative or management scheme (the Divine Dispensation or the Divine Economy) for the purpose of dispensing His life into men. The concept of dispensation primarily involves the act of distributing or dispensing. **The Divine Dispensation is God's plan, arrangement and administration to distribute and dispense His life and nature into His chosen people.** Its purpose is to accomplish the act of dispensing in order that the divine life can ultimately be dispensed into God's chosen people to regenerate, transform and bring them to glory to become sons of God.

In short, God as the Life-Giver is the source of divine dispensing. He uses the Divine Dispensation as the means to dispense His life into human beings as the recipients and beneficiaries. Divine sonship is the goal and purpose of the divine dispensing. God's intention is that through the Divine Dispensation, His life is dispensed into His chosen people, making them partakers of His life and nature. Eventually, it is to cause them to progressively mature in the divine life to attain to their status and full inheritance as sons of God.

It is also important to point out that the word "dispensation" might have different connotations and denotations to the readers as this word is closely linked to a movement called "dispensationalism" which sets forth the idea of the seven time periods called "dispensations" in God's dealing with human beings (these seven stages are: Innocency, Conscience, Human Government, Promise, Law, Grace, and Kingdom). However, as the Vine's Expository Dictionary of the New Testament Words points out, "a dispensation is not a period or epoch (a common, but erroneous, use of the word), but a mode of dealing, an arrangement, or administration of affairs."[4] Dr Charles Ryrie, in *Dispensationalism Today*, also concurred with this view and gave his proper definition of dispensation:

> A dispensation is primarily a stewardship arrangement and not a period of time (though obviously the arrangement will exist during a period of time)... A dispensation is basically the arrangement involved, not the time involved; and a proper definition will take this into account. A concise definition of a dispensation is this: 'a dispensation is a distinguishable economy in the outworking of God's purpose.'[5]

Even though the Divine Dispensation may involve successive time periods, its central thought is the divine dispensing of the life of God for the accomplishment of God's eternal purpose — the divine sonship. The different time periods involve different mode of dealings for initiating and bringing the act of the divine dispensing into completion or ultimate consummation in order to bring forth the many sons of God. Therefore, it is absolutely vital that we understand Divine Dispensation in the light and within the context of divine sonship. **Divine Dispensation has a beginning, a development and an ending for the purpose of accomplishing the goal of divine sonship.**

For the fulfillment of this eternal purpose, God has set forth different stages of the Divine Dispensation to progressively bring sonship into full realization and fruition. These successive stages are:

a)**The Stage of Initiation:** This stage involved the Father's purposeful predestination of His chosen ones unto sonship in the eternity past. There was no concept of time and space at this stage when the Father, by His foreknowledge, marked out His chosen people to become His sons according to the good pleasure of His will.

b)**The Stage of Conception:** God's plan was conceived and creation began. This stage included the period from the creation of man to the birth of the Messiah. This stage primarily involved the creation of the tripartite man in the view of the divine dispensing according to the Divine Dispensation. Throughout the Old Testament era, God's mysterious will and divine purpose were concealed in shadows and types (pointing to the good things to come) but not practically fulfilled as realities of the good things until the New Testament era.

c)**The Stage of Delivery**: In the progression of the development of God's plan for the furtherance of the Divine Dispensation, the Word became flesh and was born into the world. This stage involved everything that Christ has come to accomplish: His incarnation, crucifixion, death, resurrection and ascension. This preparatory stage of Christ's redemptive, life-releasing death and life-imparting resurrection is for the initiation and the carrying out of the next and most crucial stage of the Divine Dispensation which is the actual dispensing of the divine life into God's redeemed people.

d)**The Stage of Life, Growth & Maturity:** This stage involves the appropriation, application and administration of the accomplishment of Christ (His life-releasing death and His life-imparting resurrection) by the Spirit on the tripartite nature (spirit, soul and body) of God's chosen people according to the Father's purpose. This stage is also called *the dispensation of the Spirit* or *the dispensation of the inner life*. This commenced with the breathing of the Spirit into the disciples for regeneration of their human spirit at the night of Christ's resurrection (Jn. 20:22). It continues with the organic work of the Spirit throughout the Church age until the present, and will conclude with the glorification of the believers' body at the second coming of Christ. Since its birth on the day of Pentecost and prior to the return of Christ, the Church is entrusted with divine stewardship to carry out the dispensing function and to manage or administrate the divine dispensing for the producing of the many sons of God for fulfillment of God's eternal purpose.

e)**The Stage of Manifestation:** This involves the millennium reign of Christ on the earth where the redeemed, regenerated, transformed and glorified chosen people of God will be manifested as the sons of God, to be the joint-heirs of God and co-kings with Christ.

f)**The Stage of Consummation:** In this climactic stage, the Divine Dispensation will be brought to conclusion and completion whereby the sons of God are consummated as the New Jerusalem to become Christ's counterpart, the Lamb's wife throughout eternity.

We must take note that the Triune God in His operation of the Divine Dispensation for the divine dispensing involves three primary aspects: - (1) The Purpose of the Father, (2) the

Accomplishment of the Son, and (3) the Application by the Spirit. In the Stage of Initiation of the Divine Dispensation, the Father purposed in the eternity past to gain many sons for the fulfillment of His eternal purpose and satisfaction of His heart's desire. In the Stage of Delivery, the Son came to this earth to accomplish what was purposed by the Father. In the Stage of Life, Growth and Maturity, the Spirit applies what the Son has accomplished for the fulfillment of the Father's purpose.

In other words, in the Initiation Stage, the Father as the Source is the Initiator, the Originator, the Planner, and the Designer of the Divine Dispensation. In the Delivery Stage, the Son as the Accomplisher/Deliverer carries out what the Father has initiated, originated, planned and designed. In the Life, Growth and Maturity Stage, the Spirit as the Life-Giver applies, appropriates, administrates and executes what the Son has accomplished in His sin-redeeming, life-releasing death and life-imparting resurrection on the tripartite nature of the fallen human beings for the producing of the many sons of God.

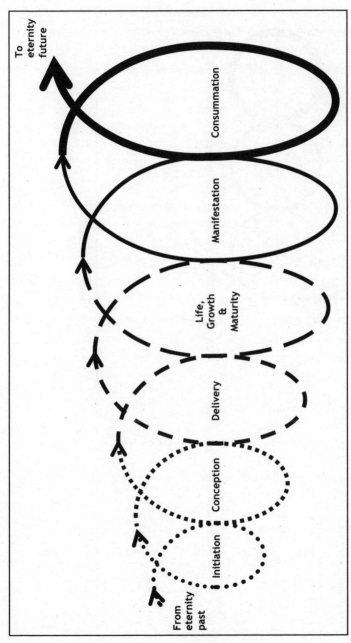

Figure 2.1: The Six Stages of the Divine Dispensation[6]

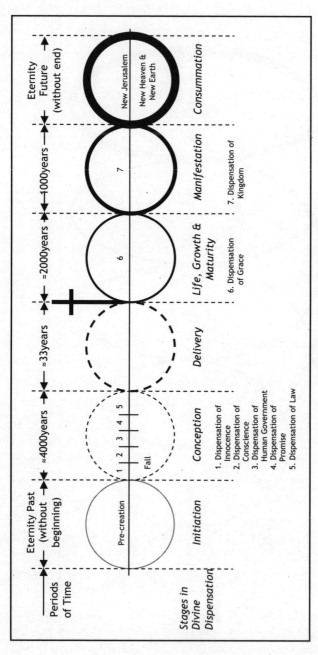

Figure 2.2: Dispensational Theology (Redefined)

The Divine Dispensing According to the Divine Dispensation

The Creation of Man as a Tripartite Being in the View of the Divine Dispensing for Divine Sonship

We have mentioned that God as the Life-Giver is the source of the divine dispensing and His chosen people are the recipients of the divine dispensing. It is therefore of utmost importance to have a biblical understanding of the make-up of man which consists of spirit, soul and body. We must understand man in the light of the divine dispensing because human being is created uniquely in God's image and likeness to be a vessel to receive the divine life.[7]

The Accomplishment of Christ and the Application or Appropriation of Christ's Accomplishment by the Spirit for the Divine Dispensing

In order to initiate the Stage of Life, Growth and Maturity in the Divine Dispensation where the life of God can be distributed and dispensed into God's chosen people, God must take two progressive and economic steps of "becoming" for the purpose of the divine dispensing. In the first "becoming" of God, the Word was made flesh and God became a man in order to bring men to God. This God-Man came to lay down His life, not merely for the sake of redeeming men from sin, but in order that men might receive the divine life (John 10:10). In the second "becoming" of God, Christ as the last Adam in resurrection became a life-giving Spirit for the initiation of the divine dispensing (Jn. 7:39; 1 Co. 15:45)[8]. The life-giving Spirit imparts the life of God into the tripartite man stage by stage in the order of the spirit, soul and body and in a progressive manner until the fallen human beings are regenerated, transformed and glorified to become the sons of God.

Hence, we see that God's plan for the divine dispensing essentially covers two important economical aspects: first, the accomplishment of Christ (His life-releasing death and His life-imparting resurrection) and second, the appropriation of the accomplishment of Christ by the Spirit. To initiate the divine dispensing, there must first be an accomplishment followed by the appropriation. While the accomplishment of Christ establishes the potential and gives us the position, the appropriation by the Spirit gives us the experience of the reality of Christ and the appropriation of the life of God in Christ Jesus. In other words, the accomplishment of Christ gives us the privilege; the appropriation by the Spirit gives us the experience.[9] The objective truth concerning the life-releasing death and life-imparting resurrection of Christ is that it can only be manifested and become ours experientially through the organic work of the Spirit inside the redeemed human beings, enabling them to appropriate and receive the divine life. Thus, the divine dispensing planned by God the Father and executed by the Son can only be appropriated by us through the activities and operations of the life-giving Spirit. Ultimately, the Holy Spirit's appropriation of Christ's accomplishment will enable the redeemed human beings to experience God's organic salvation which begins with the regeneration of the spirit, continues with the transformation of the soul and ends with the transfiguration or the redemption of the body.

We must be able to grasp and perceive that our experience of the life of Christ is only possible because of the availability of the Spirit to effectuate and appropriate the life-releasing death and life-imparting resurrection of Christ. We must receive the Holy Spirit so that He may do in us all that Christ did for us through His all-inclusive death on the cross. Until now, there has been too much doctrinal emphasis on the high privilege of God's children due to their position in Christ without a corresponding understanding of the reality of their experience in the life of Christ. In other words, there is a big discrepancy in every child of God — we have high privilege but low experience.

The inability to experience the divine dispensing of the divine life is the result of the failure to reckon and recognize two essential truths: Firstly, the ignorance that Christ in resurrection had become the life-giving Spirit for the purpose of dispensing the divine life — in order to appropriate Christ as the life of God, one must experience Christ as the life-giving Spirit. Without experiencing the Spirit, there is no appropriation of the life-releasing death and life-imparting resurrection of Christ — and therefore no realization or reality of receiving the life of God.

Secondly, ignorance towards the organic work of the Spirit on the three parts of man (spirit, soul and body). The popular dichotomous teaching (that the spirit and the soul of man are synonymous) which has been widely propagated within the Church has deprived many true seekers of God from having a genuine experience of God's organic salvation administered by the Spirit. Without proper recognition of the tripartite nature of man, there is no solid basis to appropriate and experience of God's organic salvation. The appropriation of the life of God in Christ Jesus must be experienced and manifested in a progressive manner according to the divine order of first the spirit, then the soul and finally the body. The subjective experience in the dispensing of the divine life must commence from the human spirit as the centre or base. The divine life then spreads from the spirit to reach out to the soul and finish with the body as the circumference. This way, the Spirit will bring us into the fullness of experience in the divine dispensing until all inward parts of the spirit, soul and body are filled, infused, permeated and saturated with the life of God.

The Believers in Christ as the Faithful Stewards for the Divine Dispensing

According to the New Testament, there are two denotations for the Greek word *oikonomai*. The first refers to the Divine Dispensation as we have discussed earlier. The second is in reference to the stewardship of the apostles in relation to the Divine Dispensation. Paul made known that the mystery of God's eternal will and purpose has been revealed to the holy apostles and prophets in the Spirit, and the stewardship of God's grace was given to him in order to bring to light the mystery of the Divine Dispensation concerning the Gentile believers. With his insight, Paul asserted that the mystery of Christ is that through the gospel, the Gentiles are fellow heirs and members of the body as well as fellow partakers of the promise in Christ Jesus (Eph.3:1-6).

In other words, Paul had a clear understanding that the believers are stewards of the Divine Dispensation for the purpose of divine dispensing. The Church is both a depository and a dispensing centre. We have not only rich deposits of God's grace, but are also stewards to distribute and dispense the riches of God to the many members of God's household. By the gradual dispensing of the divine life, all the inward parts of our being are nourished and built up that we might eventually be conformed to the image and likeness of Christ, becoming God's matured sons to be His complete expression and His eternal satisfaction.

As believers in Christ, we are stewards of the divine dispensing. Being stewards, we are likened to a dispensing center or a channel of supply of the divine life. We are to dispense Christ as the divine life to others for the birthing of the children of God, the building up of the Body of Christ, and the eventual bringing forth of the many sons of God.

We can use the analogy of pharmaceutical practice to illustrate this crucial truth concerning the act of dispensing. In a pharmaceutical dispensing center, medicine is dispensed to the patients according to the specific prescriptions by the doctors. By taking the prescription, the medicine with germ killing ability and immunity boosting power is dispensed into the patient, curing him from sickness and making him healthy. Spiritually, Christ is God's "medicine" or "antidote" to cure the fallen humanity. His redemptive death has the ability to eradicate and remit one's sins and His life-releasing death has the life-imparting power to revive one's spiritual health and boost one's moral standing. For this to happen, Christ as the divine "medicine" or spiritual "antidote" must be distributed and dispensed to the fallen humanity by believers in Christ who are appointed as stewards. Therefore, as stewards for the divine dispensing, we must be found faithful and trustworthy. Concerning this, Paul spoke emphatically "let a man so account of us, as of the ministers of Christ, and stewards of the mysteries of God. Moreover it is required in stewards, that a man be found faithful" (1 Co.4:1-2 NIV).

The intrinsic link between dispensation and stewardship can best be understood in the management of an ancient household where a chief stewardship is set by the owner over large estates (Lk. 16:1). In the absence of the owner, the steward was responsible to distribute the wealth of the household to its members according to the "household law" or "economies" which specified the distributions of goods. The steward was rewarded according to his faithfulness in carrying out the acts of dispensing. A trustworthy steward would faithfully carry out the distribution and dispensing of the resources for the well-being of the members of the household according to the master's wish. In the same manner, God has appointed and entrusted us the stewardship of administrating and managing the affairs of His household to dispense the unsearchable riches and inexhaustible supply of Christ to the members of the Church, which is God's house (1 Tim.3:15). What a career for every believer in Christ, that we might be a divine dispenser for the divine dispensing!

In order to be faithful stewards for the divine dispensing, we are to heed Paul's charge to Timothy against contradictory teachings to the administration or stewardship of the Divine Dispensation: "As I urged you upon my departure for Macedonia, remain on at Ephesus so that you might instruct certain men not to teach strange doctrine, nor to pay attention to myths and endless genealogies, which give rise to mere speculation rather than furthering **the administration of God** which is by faith" (1 Tim.1:3-4 NASB emphasis mine). American Standard Version (ASV) translated verse four as: "neither to give heed to fables and endless genealogies, which minister questionings, rather than **a dispensation of God** which is in faith; [so do I now]" (emphasis mine). Therefore, according to Paul, "the dispensation of God" is the focus of the New Testament ministry. The central work of the dispensation of God is to dispense God's life and attributes into His chosen people to achieve the goal of "love from a pure heart and a good conscience and a sincere faith (vs 5)", resulting in believers taking upon themselves the very nature of Christ, thus fulfilling the glorious destiny of becoming the many sons of God.

As stewards, the day will come when we will all stand before the judgment seat of Christ (2 Co. 5:10) to give an account as to whether we have ministered God's life and built

God's house according to the Divine Dispensation. On a more serious note, anything that distracts and deviates the believers from the path of Divine Dispensation is building on "wood, hay or straw" (1 Co.3:12). We may be building with wood, hay and straw when we live and work in the natural way or according to the flesh. When we build with these natural things, our work will be burned up and we will suffer loss. Warning Timothy, Paul said, "For some men, **straying from these things**, have turned aside to fruitless discussion, wanting to be teachers of the Law, even though they do not understand either what they are saying on matters about which they make confident assertions" (1 Tim.1:6-7 NASB emphasis mine).

We must therefore go according to God's divine plan — by building the household of God with "gold, silver and precious stone" (1 Co.3:12). Gold, silver, and precious stone signify our various and rich experiences of Christ through the divine dispensing so that our tripartite nature might be regenerated, transformed and glorified. As we appropriate the person of Christ and His redemptive, life-releasing and life-imparting work, what we build will stand any test and last eternally.

A Case Study of Believers as the Divine Dispensers in the Early Church

The book of Acts depicts a beautiful picture of dispensation which involves the concept of distribution and dispensing. When the church in Jerusalem was started, the twelve apostles were heavily involved in the tasks of preaching the Word (the task of divine dispensing) and the daily distribution of food to the poor and needy (the task of physical dispensing). As the church grew, the responsibilities of proclaiming the Word for the divine dispensing far outweighed the tasks of the physical dispensing of the food. In order that the apostles would not neglect the preaching of the Word for the divine dispensing, seven deacons were appointed to take care of the distribution and the dispensing of the food to the poor and the needy:-

> Acts 6:1-7 NIV
> In those days when the number of disciples was increasing, the Grecian Jews among them complained against the Hebraic Jews because their widows were being overlooked in the daily distribution of food. So the Twelve gathered all the disciples together and said, "It would not be right for us to neglect the ministry of the word of God in order to wait on tables. Brothers, choose seven men from among you who are known to be full of the Spirit and wisdom. We will turn this responsibility over to them and will give our attention to prayer and the ministry of the word." This proposal pleased the whole group. They chose Stephen, a man full of faith and of the Holy Spirit; also Philip, Procorus, Nicanor, Timon, Parmenas, and Nicolas from Antioch, a convert to Judaism. They presented these men to the apostles, who prayed and laid their hands on them. So the word of God spread. The number of disciples in Jerusalem increased rapidly, and a large number of priests became obedient to the faith.

It is significant that the deacons who were appointed for the business of distribution and dispensing of food were men of good reputation, "full of the Spirit and of wisdom." The Greek word for "full" here is *pleres*, denoting a kind of inward filling of the Spirit to fullness. The Spirit first comes to indwell and infill the spirit of the saved one, and this inward filling would subsequently overflow to the soul. To be full of the Spirit therefore means one's inward being is filled, infused, saturated and permeated with the divine life. This implies that those who are entrusted as stewards with the business of dispensing must have the quality of being full of the Spirit, even in the matter of the distribution of food — for the one who is faithful in the little task of physical dispensing of the food would also be found faithful with the great task of the spiritual dispensing of the divine life. In the physical dispensing, the table is full of the food whereas in the spiritual dispensing, the one God chooses as the divine dispenser must be full of the Spirit in order to dispense the divine life and God's riches to others.

We see that two of the deacons, Stephen and Philip, who were faithful in the serving at the table, were later promoted to become the evangelists to act as divine dispensers for the divine dispensing. Stephen, a man full of faith and power and full of the Holy Spirit (Acts 6:8;7:55), testified before the Jews and was killed, but his proclaiming of Christ became the seed that was sown into the heart of the yet converted apostle Paul — the one who was destined to become the divine dispenser to the Gentiles. Philip, another deacon, became an evangelist to Samaria and proclaimed Christ there (Acts 8:5). Both the apostles and the deacons of the early church were able to become faithful stewards for the divine dispensing because they had all served on the table and thus had a clear understanding of the true meaning and significance of the preaching of the Word, which is to dispense God's life and His riches to others. This is a marvelous revelation concerning stewardship and the task of divine dispensing. How the Lord needs more of us to be His divine dispensers in these last days!

"Receive The Food!"　　　　　　"Receive The Divine Life!"

The Physical Dispensing Vs The Divine Dispensing

Conclusion

The Divine Dispensation can be defined as "the administration or management of the divine plan and arrangement initiated by God the Father with a view to appropriating and applying the accomplished and all-inclusive death of Christ and effectuating the life-imparting resurrection of Christ by the Indwelling life-giving Spirit for the purpose of dispensing the divine life into God's tripartite elect which in the fullness of times will bring forth the sons of God for the fulfillment of God's eternal purpose and the satisfaction of the Father's heart's desire."

For the initiation of the divine dispensing according to the Divine Dispensation,[10] God has progressively revealed His hidden plan and fulfilled His purpose on a stage to stage basis (i.e. Initiation, Conception, Delivery, Life and Growth and Maturity, Manifestation and Consummation) until His goal of gaining human beings as His divine sons is fully realized.

For the administrating and managing of the divine dispensing, the Church is entrusted with the divine stewardship and the dispensing function in order to distribute and dispense the divine life and God's riches to fallen human beings and all members of God's household. As divine dispensers, believers are to administer Christ as the divine life to the sinners for their salvation and to each other for their mutual growth in life unto full maturity for the producing of the sons of God and the building up of the Body of Christ.

Through the divine dispensing, the fallen human beings will ultimately be redeemed, regenerated, transformed and glorified as the many sons of God. The Divine Dispensation in its fullness will usher in the manifestation of the sons of God for the ruling and reigning with Christ in the Millennium Kingdom and in its consummation, will bring forth the New Jerusalem as the Bride of Christ in the eternity future.

Notes II

1. The word *oikonomai* is also translated as *"plan"*, *"arrangement"*, *"administration"*,
   "stewardship" and *"economy"*. Perhaps the word economy would be a good
   term since it can be traced back to the Greek word *oikonomos*, *"one who manages
   a household"*. The terms Divine Dispensation and Divine Economy thus carry the
   same meaning.
2. http://www.ccel.org/ccel/easton/ebd2.html?term=Dispensation (access on
   15/7/2008).
3. *The American Heritage® Dictionary of the English Language, Fourth Edition.*
   Copyright © 2000 by Houghton Mifflin Company. Published by the Houghton Mifflin
   Company.
4. W.E.Vine, *Vine's Complete Expository Dictionary of Old and New Testament Words*
   (Thomas Nelson Publishers, 1996), p 174.
5. Ryrie, Charles Caldwell, *Dispensationalism Today* (Moody Press, 1975), p29,31.
6. The Divine Dispensation starts with a dotted circle to indicate that in eternity
   past, sonship was conceived in God's mind and His will on this matter was
   mysteriously hidden and veiled. It progresses to become more visible and larger
   dotted or dashed circles to indicate that God's hidden will for sonship was gradually
   unfolded and revealed, particularly by the teachings of the New Testament apostles,
   who were given the divine revelation concerning the divine sonship. In our present
   age, we can only see and know it in part until perfection comes (1 Cor. 13:9-12).
   The lines eventually become bold and continuous and form the two solid circles to
   represent the Stage of Manifestation and the Stage of Consummation to indicate that
   during the millennium and in eternity future, God's will and purpose for men will be in
   the full light and under full view, casting no shadows and leaving no doubts. The final
   circle is the boldest and largest to represent the Stage of Consummation and to
   signify that the New Jerusalem is the final product, the unique object and the ultimate
   goal of the Divine Dispensation.
7. We will discuss more concerning this subject in *"The Tripartite Man"*, *"God's Organic
   Salvation unto Sonship"* and *"The Regeneration of the Human Spirit"*.
8. We will discuss more concerning Christ as the life giving Spirit in *"The Regeneration of
   the Human Spirit"*.
9. This highly significant truth is also clearly brought out by Watchman Nee (The Spiritual
   Man, Christian Fellowship Publishers, 1977, Volume II p11):

   > *"We ought to know the relationship between the cross of Christ and
   > its application by the Spirit. The cross accomplishes all, but the Spirit
   > administers to man what it has accomplished. The cross grants us
   > position; the Holy Spirit gives us experience. The cross brings in the fact
   > of God; the Holy Spirit brings about the demonstration of that fact."*

10. It is important for readers to grasp the meaning of the terms divine dispensing and
    Divine Dispensation that are used here. The term divine dispensing means the act
    of the Spirit to dispense the life of God (zoe) into His chosen people. The term Divine
    Dispensation is used to denote God's household management, God's plan and
    God's administrative arrangement for the purpose of carrying out His plan of divine
    dispensing. The term Divine Dispensation is capitalized in order to emphasize this
    eternal PLAN and PURPOSE of God, which is to dispense His life into the redeemed
    humanity in order to gain the many sons of God for the fulfillment of His eternal
    purpose and the satisfaction of His heart's desire.

Addendum

Addendum I

The Sons of God,
Apostolic Fathers & Prophetic Mothers

One day the Lord came and asked me, "Do you know why I am restoring the apostolic and prophetic ministries in the church?"

Since I was saved in 1987, I had many wonderful moments with the Lord. Like the disciples walking down the road to Emmaus, the Lord came and walked along with me, explaining the scriptures and sharing His heart to me. When I was young in faith, it took a long time (even years) for me to grasp what the Lord revealed to me as my learning and understanding was slow. Now that I am older and more mature in faith, it is much easier for me to grasp what He is saying. The divine revelations and biblical insights contained in *The Sons of God* series are the golden nuggets that I picked up along the journey as I was walking alone with Him.

He shared with me — Spirit to spirit, Mind to mind, and Heart to heart. Many times I was so filled with the inspired thoughts that my spirit and heart leapt for joy. Occasionally, sensing that His teaching anointing was near, I would try to ask those mysterious questions in search for the answer. He would reply if I asked rational and sensible questions, but would also keep silent if the opportune time had not come for me to know. But if the question I asked was nonsense, He would keep silent or even withdraw Himself (like asking: "A good God will not send sinners to hell, will He?"). He was never there with me to satisfy my curiosity or to answer all my doubts. Something will remain a secret until we meet Him face to face. "For now we see in a mirror, dimly, but then face to face. Now I know in part, but then I shall know just as I also am known" (1 Co.13:12). I had learnt to be attentive in spirit to listen to Him when He spoke. "The Lord came and stood there, calling as at the other times, "Samuel! Samuel!" Then Samuel said, "Speak, for your servant is listening." (1 Sam. 3:10).

This is the last days. The Lord will recover the foundational truth to the church so that we may know Him more fully. "The secret things belong to the Lord our God, but the things revealed belong to us and to our children forever, that we may follow all the words of this law" (Dt.29:29). He is looking for those who would listen to Him and linger with Him, to reveal to them secrets and mysteries of the kingdom. "And you will know the truth, and the truth will set you free" (Jn. 8:32). The restoration and recovery of these fundamental truths will equip the church to be more fully prepared for His soon coming.

When the Lord asked me, "Do you know why I am restoring the apostolic and prophetic ministries in the church?", my mind began to flip through passages of scriptures concerning the ministries of the apostles and the prophets. I did find some scriptural references on the subject. So I replied, "Lord, it is because you want to reveal and unfold the divine mystery, for your Word said that the mystery of Christ is revealed by the Spirit to God's holy apostles and prophets" (Eph.3:4-5). "Yes," the Lord replied, "the 21st century church is the church that must move in revelation knowledge. The new wine cannot be poured into the old wineskins (Mk. 2:22). An apostolic and prophetic church is the new wineskin for Me to contain and pour forth my new wine."

"What else?" He asked. I was quick to give my second

answer, "It is because the house of God is built on the foundation of the apostles and prophets, with You Yourself as the chief cornerstone" (Eph.2:19-20). "That is true also," replied the Lord, "For I am now shaking Christendom. The leaven of abominable teachings I will remove (1 Co.5:7), and the heretical wines that intoxicate my people I will judge (Rev.17:2), until what is unshakable remains (Heb.12:26-27). The apostolic teachings and prophetic revelations will remain until I come, for these are the building materials for the foundation of My House."

"Is there anything else?" the Lord continued to ask. Pondering for a while, knowing that He wanted to give me understanding, I replied, "Lord. I don't know. Please show me." He said, "I am restoring the apostles and the prophets because I am restoring the image of the Father to My children. For that to happen, I need sons." Having gained much understanding concerning God's sons after writing *The Call to Sonship*, I have a better comprehension of what the Lord taught me on that day.

The Lord said that the purpose of His coming to the earth was to express and represent the Father. "There are two aspects concerning the Father's work. He is the Father of Creation as well as the Father of Regeneration. As the Father of Creation, He is the Source, the Originator and the Creator of all things. Nothing comes into existence without the Father's will, for all things are created for His good pleasure."

"When the Father first created the angelic beings, they were called the sons of God. The angels witnessed the creation of physical world and shouted for joy when they saw the marvelous work of creation through God's spoken words (Job 38:7)."

"When Adam was created, he became the closest resemblance of the Father's image and likeness (Gen.1:26-27). As a created human son, Adam could be a better expression and representation of the Father in comparison to the created angelic sons or any other created creatures. For this reason the Father gave the dominion of the earth to His created human son (Gen.1:28)."

"People have no idea how the Father loves His creatures. It is impossible for one creature to appreciate and have concern for another creature as God has. That is why I said, "Are not two sparrows sold for a penny? Yet not one of them will fall to the ground apart from the will of your Father (Mt.10:29)." To men, the sparrows are of little worth. To God, He is their Father. Could you understand the singing of birds early in the morning? Yet their songs are sweet to the Heavenly Father, for they are praising God for His provision and protection."

"No one could express and represent the Father more fully and completely than His only begotten Son. Why? He is the Son. Only a son could express a father, just as a servant could speak on his master's behalf. But a servant could not express the heart of a father, and a father needs a son to express himself. All the saints and prophets in the Old Testament could speak for God but could not speak for the Father (though some did have a glimpse of the Father's heart of God). They were the servants, not sons. They pointed people to God as the Creator, the Master, the LORD but rarely made Him known as the Father."

"For this reason in the fullness of time the Father sent His eternal begotten Son into the world. Hebrews 1:1-2 says that "In the past God spoke to our forefathers through the prophets at many times and in various ways, but in these last days He has spoken to us by His Son". The Son is the brightness of His glory and the express image of His person. The Son made the Father known. If you want to know the Father, you must know the Son."

"While on this earth, as the only begotten Son, I made known the Father of Creation. When the disciples said to me, "Lord, teach us to pray", I told them: "When you pray, say "Our Father in heaven" (Lk.11:2). I showed them that men are to trust the Father of Creation for their daily provision and to learn from the birds of the air, for if the Heavenly Father feeds them, how much more He cares for men created in His own image? (Mt.6:26). While on this earth, I had revealed the Father of Creation as the Father in heaven. As God's created creatures, men could pray to the Father in heaven for help to meet their needs."

"From the beginning, the Father already loved Adam deeply as a father loves a son. Adam was created with the potential to become His genuine son. The created human life, though on the lower plane, could join to the uncreated divine life on the higher plane. All creatures could know God as the Father of Creation, but only human beings are given the privilege to experience God as the Father of Regeneration."

"When His created son sinned and hid himself among the trees of the garden, the Father came and looked for him – like a father searching for his son. Today, all the created sons of God had fallen. But the Father of Creation still looking and searching for His lost sons. Like the waiting father in the story of the prodigal son, My Father is always waiting for sinners to come home (Lk.15:11-32)."

"To redeem the lost created sons and to gain the genuine sons that share His uncreated eternal life, the Father unfolded His plans and shared His heart's desire to a man from Ur of the

Chaldeans. This man Abram was without a son. But the Father said to Abram (when he was ninety-nine years old), "I am El-Shaddai, walk before My face, and be perfect (Gen. 17:1)". The Father told him that He is the God of udders, the Almighty God with breasts [Note: *Shaddai* is related to the noun *shad*, means "breast" or "udder"]. For the Father to fulfill His purpose to regenerate, nurture and feed His many created sons to transform them to become His genuine sons, He must be the God of udders to them. For this reason the Father must give Abram a son, for out of the loin of this son, God's eternal begotten Son in the fullest of time shall come to take the human form to accomplish the Father's eternal purpose."

"God wanted Abram to know He was not contended just being the Father of Creation, He wanted to become the Father of Regeneration for all His created human sons. Though they had fallen, the Father will provide a way to redeem them. At the place where Abraham later sacrificed his son, the Father revealed that near this place His begotten Son will be sacrificed as a Lamb to redeem His fallen sons. Abraham rejoiced at the thought of seeing my day; he saw it and was glad (Jn. 8:56)."

"So the Father changed Abram's name to Abraham. You know that when there is a change of name of a person, there is a change of character, purpose and destiny of that person. Abram means exalted father; he was among the greatest men of the east at that time. Abram is a type of the Father of Creation. The Father of Creation is highly exalted and greatly feared by all His creatures. Abraham, on the other hand, means the father of many. When the Father changed Abram's name to Abraham, He was revealing to Abram that even though He was (and still is) an exalted Father in heaven before His creation, more than anything, His deepest heart's desire is to assume the role of a begetting Father i.e. to become a Father of multitude and a Father of many nations."

"My disciple John was caught up in heaven and saw a great multitude that no one could count, from every nation, tribe, people and language, standing before the throne of the Father and in front of the Lamb (Rev.7:9). It is the Father's good pleasure to give His many redeemed, regenerated, transformed, and glorified sons the kingdom and the inheritance, which was ordained and prepared for them before the foundation of the world (Lk. 12:32, Eph.1:3-4). That is what the Father meant when He said, "He who overcomes will inherit all this, and I will be his God and he will be my son (Rev.21:7)."

"As the eternal begotten Son, I had revealed and made known the Father's name to those whom He gave me out of the world (Jn. 17:6). They had known the Father as their Father in heaven, but they had yet to know the Father as their Abba Father. After resurrection, I was begotten by the Father in My humanity to be the Firstborn Son among many brothers (Acts 13:33; Rom.8:29). Before I was resurrected, I called them servants and friends (Jn. 15:14). After my resurrection, I called them my brothers (Jn. 20:17). As the Firstborn, I have many brothers."

"After designated as the Firstborn Son, I enter the second phase of My ministry in order to manifest and make known the Abba Father (Father of Regeneration). The first phase of My ministry is to make known the Heavenly Father, Father of Creation, and the second phase of My ministry is to make known Abba Father, the Father of Regeneration. You have noted that I prayed to My Father this way: "Righteous Father... .I have made you known to them, and will continue to make you known in order that the love you have for me may be in them and that I myself may be in them" (Jn. 17:25-26). As the Firstborn Son, it is my desire and purpose to reveal the Abba Father."

"I could make known the Father of Creation to the fallen creatures, but I could only make known the Father of Regeneration to those who are genuinely begotten by the Father. In other words, only those who are born of God and born of the Spirit (Jn. 1:13; 3:8) could know the Father of Regeneration. The Father of Creation creates and the Father of Regeneration begets. The created things are the creatures or creation of God. The begetting ones are the children of God. Whilst the Father of Creation calls His created ones "sons", the Father of Regeneration calls His begetting ones "children". He calls them "sons" when the children grow up into maturity in the divine life to manifest and express the Father's character. You had understood Me well and had managed to make a clear distinction between the children of God and the sons of God in your writing *The Call to Sonship*."

"You have heard Me said that only a son could make a father known. Truly no one knows the Father except the Son, and no one comes to the Father except through Me (Lk.10:22; Jn.14:6). That's why I told Philip "If you really knew Me, you would know my Father as well, for anyone who has seen Me has seen the Father" (Jn. 14:7,9). Yes, the Son is the radiance of God's glory and exact representation of His being (Heb.1:3). To know the Father of Glory, you have to know the Son."

"As the Firstborn Son, it is even now my responsibility to continue to make the Father (of Regeneration) known to His children and My brothers in order to bring many sons to glory. (Heb.2:10). That is why I said, "I will declare your name to my brothers; in the presence of the congregation I will sing your praises" (Heb.2:12)."

After a long discourse with the Lord, I could sense His burden and earnest desire to make the Father known to His children. Yet I could not link what He said to the question He first asked concerning the restoration of the apostles and prophets in the last days. Knowing my thoughts, He told me, "Be patient, I am about to reveal to you the reason and purpose for the restoration of the ministries of apostles and prophets in these last days."

"As the Son, I express all that the Father has and is, for I am in the Father and the Father in Me, and I and the Father are One (Jn. 10:30; 14:11). Therefore, I do what the Father does (Jn. 10:37). I do nothing on my own but speak just what the Father has taught me (Jn. 8:28). I never speak of my own accord, but the Father who sent me commanded me what to say and how to say it (Jn.12:49). Concerning Me, Isaiah said, "He will be called....Everlasting Father" (Isa.9:6). You had heard Me said just now that I will declare the Father's name to My brothers (Heb.2:12), yet I also said, "Here am I, and the children God has given me" (Heb.2:13). The Son and the Father are eternally one — we are distinct but not separable. I am the Firstborn Son, yet the children of God are also My children. The Father has made Me the Firstborn Brother, He has also given Me the children of God."

"It has been said that "Moses was faithful as a servant in all God's house....But Christ is faithful as a son over God's house" (Heb.3:5-6). The children of God are God's house. They (today's preachers) had said that the five-fold ministries — apostles, prophets, evangelists, pastors and teachers — are My servants and My representatives to rule over God's house. Many apostles today have even said that they had been given the mandate by Me to govern and rule over My house and to put My House in order."

"As I told you earlier, the Father wants sons, not servants. A servant could express a master but only a son could express a father. I had many "Moses" who serve Me faithfully in My house. But where are My sons?"

The Lord paused for a moment, His eyes streamed with tears. "I need sons, and I need fathers and mothers in My House. I need the Abraham-s (the fathers of multitude) and the Sarah-s (the mothers of multitude). I need apostolic fathers and prophetic mothers!"

"I am not saying that I do not need servants. True servants are sons, like My dear apostles Paul and John. Sons could become true servants, but servants could not become true sons. True servanthood transforms God's children into sons, and true sons are servants. Likewise, servants could not become My friends and brothers, only true sons could become My friends and brothers. True sons are My brothers, friends and servants; they are ones that truly know the Father, for I make known My Father to them."

"In the 50's, 60's and 70's, I had restored the ministries of the evangelists and the pastors-teachers. In the 80's and 90's, I began to restore prophets and apostles. It is now the 21st Century, and I am consolidating the ministries of apostles, prophets, evangelists and pastors-teachers in preparation for the final and the climax move on earth — the movement of the sons of God! This final movement on earth will bring the Church to her full maturity and stature as the sons of God to usher in My return."

"The evangelists and pastors-teachers have served their functions well. But the apostles and prophets are still aligning and positioning themselves to serve their role in My House. For them to align perfectly with My will and My purpose, they need to know My heart beat at this hour. This is why I am speaking to you today. This is why I have given you the vision and the burden to write the book *The Sons of God* for Me. This book will help My people, in particular My apostles and prophets, to divinely align and position themselves to fulfill the calling of their Father."

"The evangelists reveal Me as a Savior, Healer and Deliverer. The pastors-teachers made known My role as a Shepherd. They all could express and represent the Father in a limited sense. But much grace is upon the apostles and prophets to express and represent the Father more accurately, completely and fully — for they laid the foundation of My Father's House (Eph.2:20), and to them are given the revelations of the mysteries of My Father's heart's desire and His eternal purpose (Eph.1:9;3:4-5)."

"You have heard Me said, "All things have been committed to me by My Father. No one knows the Son except the Father, and no one knows the Father except the Son and those to whom the Son chooses to reveal him" (Mt.11:27). The apostles and prophets are dear to My heart. They are my closest brothers. They are the chief sons. Now that they are coming forth and are becoming more mature, I will reveal and manifest the Father more and more to them. Then they too will reveal and make known the Father more and more to their fellow brothers and the children of God. When all My brothers and children have full and accurate knowledge of the Son of God, — by experiencing Me and comprehending fully what I say and do — they too will have full, accurate and comprehensive knowing and experiencing of their Father. In this way, they will attain oneness in the faith and become mature, attaining to the measure of the stature of My fullness (Eph.4:13)."

"You have heard Me said, "Elijah does indeed come first to restore all things" (Mt.17:11, Mk. 9:12). Yes, John the Baptist came in the spirit and power of Elijah. He came to prepare the way and to make ready for Me a people prepared (Mt.3:3; Isa. 40:3; Lk. 1:17). Yet John the Baptist was an Elijah-forerunner prepared the way for My first coming. The company of the apostles and prophets are the last days Elijah-forerunners to prepare the way and to make ready a people prepared for My second coming. They are the fulfillment of Malachi 4:5-6 prophecy. These Elijah-forerunners are to restore the hearts of the fathers to their children and the hearts of the children to their fathers. How could the fathers turn to their children and the children turn to their fathers unless My apostles and prophets reveal, make known and manifest the Father to them? The heart of My children must first turn to My Father before restoration of all things could take place."

"The apostles and prophets inherit the double portion of the spirit of Elijah. How did Elisha receive the double portion? He fixed his eyes on Elijah. When Elijah went up to heaven in a whirlwind, Elisha saw this and cried out, "My father! My father!" (2 Ki.2:9-15). The apostles and prophets received their double portion by fixing their eyes on their Father. This double portion of the prophetic and apostolic mantles are the most precious gifts of My Father to My Church in order that God's children might also know and love the Father and would call their Father from the depth of their spirit, crying "Abba, Father!""(Rom.8:15).

"For the apostles and prophets to manifest the Father, they must mature to become God's chief sons just as I became the Firstborn Son to make the Father known. They must be among the first to partake of the Father's life and nature and grow into maturity as His sons. Apostles and prophets, if they pursue life (the life of God) and not gifts, powers, position and prestige (if they do so, they would disqualify themselves), they will be among the company and assembly of the first-born who are enrolled in heaven (Heb.12:23). It is My Father's will that they should be counted as the firstfruits among the 144000 (Rev.14:3-4), and become the early overcomers or the company of the man-son who are to rule all nations with a rod of iron (Rev.12:5). By their humility, obedience and maturity, they will be entrusted (together with all God's matured sons) with the Father's blessings, and to fully represent Him to run the affairs of their Father on this earth."

"By maturing as God's sons, they (apostles and prophets) also become the fathers and mothers to My children. I am raising apostolic fathers and prophetic mothers in the last days to mature and equip My Church. Take heed that I did not say I raise fatherly apostles and motherly prophets, but apostolic fathers and prophetic mothers. The apostles and prophets, in their most noble function and highest capacity, must act as spiritual fathers and mothers. Because they are chief sons — ones who partake of the Father's nature and character more fully — they could express and make known more precisely, correctly, thoroughly and fully the Abba Father — the El-Shaddai, the God of udders — in order that God's begetting children might be nourished with the rich and bountiful supply of the divine life. In this way, all God's children could know and experience the Father to the extent that they eventually grow and mature in the divine life, conforming to My image, coming into My full stature, and becoming the sons of God."

"My Father reserves the double portion anointing for His

chief sons, who will be the last days Elijah-forerunners. What is this double portion anointing? It is the gifts of fatherhood and motherhood. It is to raise a company of apostolic fathers and prophetic mothers."

"True prophets are recognized by demonstration of sonship and motherhood, and the authentic test to apostleship is sonship and fatherhood. You have heard Me said: real sons are My brothers, friends and servants. But real sons are fathers and mothers too! True apostles and prophets are spiritual fathers and mothers that could produce spiritual children and sons. You could learn this from the life of My dear apostles Paul and John: They are sons to God, yet fathers and mothers to God's children!" (Scriptural references: 1 Co.4:14,15, 17; 2 Co.12:14; Gal.4:19; Phil.2:22; 1 Th. 2:7; 1 Tim.1:2, 18; Tit.1:4; Phm.1:10; 1 Jn. 2:1,12,13,18,28; 3:7,18 ; 4:4; 5:21).

"The apostolic and prophetic movement is bringing forth the sons of God movement, which is the greatest sign of the Century of the nearness of My coming. My Father is waiting for His children to come to full sonship and to reach full maturity to usher in and hasten My return; and I am coming soon to complete their redemption, to consummate their transformation, and to commence the millennial reign. Tell My people to get ready!"

(A Discourse with Jesus in May 2009)

Addendum Ii

Was Adam a son of God?

Luke 3:38 "...Adam, the son of God." (Original text reads as "...Adam, of God.")

In the beginning, God had three angelic sons. The first was Lucifer, the second Michael, and the third Gabriel. These three archangels were brothers.

The eldest angelic son, Lucifer, had fallen and became Satan, or the Devil. From henceforth, he was no longer a brother to the two archangels. He was their enemies. He was God's enemy.

When God created the physical world, a human son came into existence. His name was Adam, which means "a man". He was not an angelic son, for he did not live an angelic life. He lived a human life.

"How different was this human son compared to the angelic sons?"

Obviously, this human son could reproduce his own kind but the angelic sons could neither marry nor be given in marriage (Gen.1:28; Mt.22:30). (The exception was in the days of Noah. It was said that "the sons of God saw that the daughters of men were beautiful, and they married any of them they chose" (Gen.6:2). The inter-mingling of fallen angels with humans beings gave birth to monstrous offspring called the Nephilim).

The distinction between the human son and the angelic sons (which is of our interest) was this: Adam could live in both the physical and spiritual realms simultaneously, but the angels could only live in the unseen, spiritual realm (though they occasionally by God's permission do appear in temporary human form—see Gen.18:2; Heb.13:2). This means that Adam could come into contact with and substantiate both the physical and spiritual world. His eyes could see the wonders of nature; his ear could hear the singing of birds; his nose could smell the fragrance of a flower; his mouth could enjoy the fruits of the trees (and so many of them with varieties of taste...I wonder whether he had ever tried that durian?!); and his body could sense the heat and the cold. Yet at the same time, his spirit could sense God's presence. He could even see the form of God. They talked to one another. They enjoyed each other presence.

But one day, another tragic took place. This human son had fallen too. He listened to the fallen angel and ate that forbidden fruit.

An angelic son had fallen. A human son had fallen too.

"What were God's responses? How did God deal with them?"

When the angelic son fell, God expelled him from the Mount of God, from the Garden of God (Eze.28:13,16). This fallen angel was cast down to the earth (Isa.14:12). And when the human son fell, God drove him out of the Garden of Eden. With a flaming sword flashed back and forth, this fallen human son could no longer return to the Garden he once loved (Gen.3:24).

"It seems like God was fair, for in His judgment He did not

show favoritism to either His angelic son or His human son. Both were banished from His presence."

However, God did something unusual to His fallen human son. He slew a lamb and made garments of skin to cloth this fallen human son and his wife (Gen.3:21).

"Did Adam know the meaning of this gracious deed of God?"

Yes, he did. He named his wife Eve, which means "life" or "living". Somehow, I think Adam knew God had a divine Son; and one day, this divine Son would come to take the human form to die as the Lamb of God to redeem him and all his descendents from their sins and transgressions.

"What about that angelic son? Didn't God give him a chance to repent? Anyway, would he ever repent if this chance was given to him?"

No, my friend, he has no chance (and even if he is given a chance to repent now, he will not, for he does not know what repentance is. As a blind man does not know what seeing is, so the fallen angels will never know what repenting means). When the angelic sons sinned against God (one third in number), they were utterly cast out of heaven without room for repentance. The Devil and these angels are cursed and doomed for destruction. An everlasting fire is prepared for them and awaiting them (Mt.25:41). One day, Satan himself will be thrown into the lake of burning sulfur. There, he will be tormented day and night for ever and ever (Rev.20:10).

But God's fallen human son and the rest of his descendants have a chance, if they choose to accept what God has to offer --by repenting from their sins and turning to God for salvation. God had already prepared a salvation plan for them. We called this plan "the Good News" -- and this gospel of salvation is for fallen human beings only and not for fallen angels.

"But I thought I just said that for God to be fair He must not show favoritism. Isn't God a righteous Judge? Why He did not offer the Good News to the fallen angels also? After all, they were His sons. After all, both had rebelled, sinned and fallen."

Wait, my friend. Before you jump to conclusion that God was unfair in His judgment, we must pause for a moment and ask, "What does God really want? What was in His mind when He brought forth His angelic sons and His human son into being?"

When God created the angelic sons, they had different ranking: archangels, seraphim, cherubim and angels. Lucifer as God's first angelic son was created full of wisdom and perfect in beauty, with every precious stone as his covering (Eze.28:12-14). But whether it is an archangel or a low ranking angel, God's work on them was finished when He created them.

This was not so for God's human son, Adam. When God created Adam, His work on him was yet to be completed. His intention was to make Adam a divine-human son. That was why God placed His human son in front of the tree of life. God's intention was that by partaking of the fruit of the tree of life, Adam would receive God's life and become His divine-human son.

Even though God's human son was made a little lower than the angelic sons (Ps.8:5; Heb.2:9 -- for the plane of human is lower than the plane of angels), the human son was created with the potential to live in a plane even higher than angelic plane -- the plane of God. God has prepared a divine destiny for His human sons -- to share in His life, nature, authority and power. Because the human son could partake of the life of God, he could be transformed into divine-human son to have authority over the angels. The angels are servants to the divine-human sons (Heb.1:14). The day will come when the saints (as the true sons of God) will judge the fallen angels (1 Co.6:3).

Do not be surprised of the saying that God wants divine-human sons. Angelic sons could not satisfy God. Human sons would never make God happy. This means that after God created His angelic sons, He was unsatisfied. But even after He had brought forth a human son, Adam, God was still unsatisfied. God will not be satisfied until He gains His many divine-human sons.

"But I would think that God was unsatisfied and unhappy because His human son, Adam, had disappointed Him through his rebellion. I would think that he could have made God happy -- if he had continued to live a perfect, sinless human life and do whatever God asked him to do."

No, my friend, God would still be unsatisfied even if Adam had lived a blameless human life. Likewise, God will not be pleased with you today even if you try to live righteously -- trying to keep the commandments with all your human strength and to the best of your abilities. Of course, I can confidently say this: you will fail to live righteously if you really try. For in God's eyes, all our righteous acts are like filthy rags (Isa.64:6). And if you do sincerely want to live a blameless life (all by yourself and without God's help), make sure that you don't break any of the laws. For it is said, "For whoever keeps the whole law and yet stumbles at just one point is guilty of breaking all of it"

(Jas. 2:10).

"If living a righteous life cannot please God, how can I please Him? What does God really want from me?"

As I said earlier, God wants divine-human sons. Neither angelic sons nor human sons satisfy God. God's plan and purpose is to gain for Himself divine-human sons. God wants you and I to become His divine-human sons.

"Does that mean that God wants to make us demigods -- half god and half human, like the Nephilim?"

Nope. Demigods are the union of angelic and human lives. This inter-mingling of different lives or species is abhorred and prohibited by God. It is said, "Do not plant two kinds of seed in your vineyard; if you do, not only the crops you plant but also the fruit of the vineyard will be defiled" (Dt.22:9). Such forbidden union would bring forth defiled species -- like the Nephilim. For this reason God sent deluge in Noah's days to judge and terminate the defiled race.

Divine-human sons share both the divine life and the human life. They are the union of God and men (God-men). They possess both divinity and humanity. Adam had human life, but he did not have the divine life. The first person on earth who became a divine-human son was the Lord Jesus. From the beginning, He was the eternal begotten divine Son (Jn. 3:16). He was with the Father in the beginning (Jn. 1:2). The world was created by Him and through Him (Jn. 1:3; Heb.1:2). Two thousand years ago, He was conceived in the womb of a virgin and born in a manger as a human being. Though He was God, He did not demand and cling to His rights as God. Instead, He made Himself nothing and took the humble position of a slave and appeared in human form and born into the world (Phil. 2:6-7). Through His incarnation, this divine Son became a divine-human Son. He united divinity to humanity. The Son of God became a man to enable men to become sons of God. Through our union with Him, we too could become divine-human sons. The genuine sons of God are divine-human sons, possessing both divinity and humanity. These divine-human sons called sons of God are ones that satisfy the Father's heart and fulfill His eternal purpose.

"Wait a minute. I thought you said that God's angelic sons and God's human son (Adam) are sons of God too. Now there is a new species that come forth, the divine-human species or God-men kind, which are also called the sons of God. If all of them are God's sons, don't they share equal status and enjoy same privilege before God?"

The divine-human sons are God's true sons. They are God's heirs. Angels and Adam were God's sons because God is their Creator, Source, or Originator (father denotes the source or origin). We could say that Adam was God's created son. But we could not say that Adam was God's regenerated son. Adam could call God "Father (of Creation)", but he could not address God as "Abba (Father of Regeneration)". Only those human beings that are born of God could genuinely be called sons of God because God is genuinely their begetting Father.

"Who then was the first fallen son of Adam that became a genuine son of God possessing both divine and human nature?"

I believe it was Peter. Something happened to him at the night of Christ's resurrection. The risen Lord breathed on him (and others with him) and said, "Receive the Holy Spirit"

(Jn. 20:22). When Peter received the Holy Spirit, he received the impartation of divine life. In his own words, he said, "I have become a partaker of the divine nature" (2 Pe. 1:4).

"Wasn't this act of God similar to what God did to Adam? The Bible says, "The Lord God formed the man from the dust of the ground and breathed into his nostrils the breath of life, and the man became a living being (Gen.2:7)."

No. This second breath was different from the first breath. God created the human spirit with His first breath, but God regenerates the human spirit with His second breath. In the first breath, the human spirit was created to become the vessel to contain the second breath (the zoe life). The first breath made Adam a human son. The second breath made Peter a divine-human son.

This second breath is the miracle of born again or regeneration, and is an absolute necessity for those who want to become genuine sons of God.

You see, God is Spirit (Jn.4:24). He is the Father of our spirits (Heb.12:9). It is only in our spirit that we become the offspring of God. For one to become God's genuine son, he must be born of God, for that which is born of flesh is flesh, and that which is born of the Spirit is spirit (Jn. 3:6). You cannot become God's son by own efforts; neither could you enter God's Kingdom as an orphan. You must be born of God. John 1:12-13 says, "Yet to all who received him, to those who believed in his name, he gave the right to become children of God -- children born not of natural descent, nor of human decision or a husband's will, but born of God." You enter the Father's House as His begetting child.

And that was exactly what happened to Peter at the night of

Christ's resurrection. He was born again in spirit. Yes, he was the first human being who was born again in spirit! He was the first fallen son of Adam to partake of the divine life and nature.

You, my friend, could become the next Peter, the next divine-human son of God, if you want to. This miracle could happen to you right now if you would pray with me:

"Lord Jesus, thank you for dying for my sins. Come into my life and breathe into me the Breath of Life. Thank you for your salvation to enable me to become a genuine son of God."

Friend, if you had said that prayer, I believe you have been born again. You have something that Adam did not have. You have the life of God residing in you. That makes you a genuine son of God.

So, what do you think? Was Adam a son of God?

(PS In this discussion, we try to bring out the difference between angelic son, human son and divine-human son. God's true sons must be redeemed, regenerated, transformed and glorified. We will address this more fully in Book 2 of The Sons of God Series with the title "The Tripartite Man, The Fall & The Organic Salvation").

Addendum Iii

What the Pattern Son Jesus and other Sons of God have in Common

All believers born in spirit are prospective sons of God. This sonship will be realized and fully manifested when we mature to fullness in the divine life and conform to the glorious image and likeness of the firstborn Son, Jesus. The greatest evidences that the functional sons of God are coming forth are the demonstration, expression and manifestation of the earthly living, working, walking, and acting of believers according to the pattern of the model Son, Christ, the firstborn among many brothers.

There are many commonalities between Jesus as the firstborn Son and His many brothers that He will bring to glory. We must live, conduct and regulate ourselves according to these yardsticks — taking Christ as our pattern and type that we must conform to — if we want to progress to become the functional and fully mature sons of God.

The following are the compelling comparisons and striking similarities between the Pattern Son and other sons of God:

The divine-human living
While on the earth for thirty-three and a half years, the Lord Jesus possessed both the divine life and the human life. He was totally God and totally man. Yet He did not live by His sinless human life. If the Lord had lived by the human life, He would have lived a perfect, spotless life because His human life was without sin and moral defect. However, the Lord did not come in order to live a perfect human life or to show

us how to live our human life. He came so that we might have the divine life and live by this life (Jn.10:10). Since the children of God are the recipients of the divine life, the Lord showed them how to live, work, walk and act according to the highest life resides deep within their spirit. For this reason the Lord denied His perfect human life and lived by the life of the Father within Him. In other words, His human life lived in subjection and subjugation to His divine life. The Lord lived to express the divine life, nature and attributes in His human living.

Because He lived by the divine life, He could live, work, walk, and act in line with the will and purpose of God the Father. His disciple John personally witnessed how the Lord lived by the Father (Jn.6:57). His working was the Father's working: "My Father is always at His work to this very day, and I, too, am working" (5:17). His acting was the Father's acting: "the Son can do nothing by Himself; He can do only what He sees His Father doing, because whatever the Father does the Son also does" (5:19). His speaking was the Father's speaking: "For I did not speak of My own accord, but the Father who sent Me commanded Me what to say and how to say it" (12:49). His willing was the Father's willing: "My food is to do the will of Him who sent Me, and to finish His work" (4:34). The Lord lived such a life of total dependence on the Father that He said, "By Myself I can do nothing" (5:30).

All prospective God's sons live the divine-human living according to the Lord's pattern. As He lived by the divine life in His human living, so we must also live by that life: "Just as the living Father sent Me and I live by (through, because of) the Father, even so whoever continues to feed on Me [whoever takes Me for his food and is nourished by Me] shall [in his turn] live through and because of Me" (6:57 AMP).

By living out the divine life in their human living, these sons live a life that expresses, manifests and demonstrates the Father's nature, character and attributes. By such a divine-human living, others will be drawn, attracted and captivated to know and experience Christ for themselves.

Live by and walk according to the human spirit

The Lord Jesus while on this earth lived and walked according to His human spirit. As His spirit was alive, He could live in both realms — the realm of God and the realm of men — at the same time: "No one has ascended to heaven but He who came down from heaven, that is, the Son of Man who is in heaven" (Jn.3:13). His physical body was on the earth, yet His spirit was in constant communication and fellowship with the Father in heaven. He told Nathanael, "I tell you the truth, you shall see heaven open, and the angels of God ascending and descending on the Son of Man" (Jn. 1:51). The Lord's spirit was the reality of Jacob's ladder that joined earth to heaven and heaven to earth.

As the Lord had a strong and vibrant spirit, He could move by revelation, perception, and intuition. He could perceive things that were incomprehensible by the natural mind. He could see Nathanael while he was still under the fig tree before Philip called him (Jn.1:48); he could look at the Samaritan woman and tell her that she had five husbands (Jn.4:18); He could discern whether a sickness was originated from demons or by natural causes (Mt.17:18; Mk. 9:25); He could apprehend the thoughts and motives and conditions of the heart of men (Lk.9:47; Jn.2:24; Mt.9:4), and He could perceive the things to come (Mt.16:21).

The prospective God's sons are born of God and regenerated in their spirit (Jn.1:13; 3:6). Like the pattern Son, their regenerated spirit is the reality of Jacob's ladder that connects them to the heavenly realm. Possessing strong and matured spirit, they could worship the Father in spirit and truth (Jn. 4:23); they could see and hear and perceive things that others could not (Mt.16:17; Ac.5:3; 8:20); they could know the things to come (Jn.16:13); and they could do greater things than what the Lord did (Jn.14:12).

The Lord moved and lived and had His being in His spirit. His spirit was sensitive to the needs of the people around Him (Jn.11:33; Mt.9:36, 14:14; 15:32, 20:34). His spirit often led Him to places where the Father's will and purpose could be accomplished (Mk. 10:33; Jn. 4:4-7). The prospective sons of God must live and move and have their being in their spirit too — for the regenerated human spirit is where the Spirit dwells and is the source of newness of life and power. One of the most distinguishable commonality between the Firstborn Son and His many brothers is that they live a life that is led, ruled, regulated and governed by their human spirit.

A loving relationship with the Father

God is our Father as much as He is the Lord's own Father. He is our Abba as well as the Lord's Abba (Mk.14:36; Rom.8:15). Abba loves us as much as He loves Jesus. The Father Himself loves us dearly because we are His begetting children (Jn.16:27). 1 John 3:1 says, "How great is the love the Father has lavished on us, that we should be called children of God! And that is what we are!"

The Lord loved the Father so supremely and sacrificially that He would not do anything that was not in line with the Father's will. Even if it meant to lay down His own life, He was willing to become obedient to the Father, even death on the cross (Mt.26:39; Jn.10:17-18; Phil.2:8). Motivated by the love for the Father, the Lord willfully submitted His life to accomplish God's purpose for His life (Lk.23:46).

The prospective God's sons have a passionate love for their Father. They are dedicated wholly, utterly and unreservedly to God to do His will and to glorify Him only. Their deep, full, complete personal experience and knowledge of the love of God qualify and enable them to act as fathers and mothers in God's house — to nurture and bring forth the younger ones. These sons could love the Father so sacrificially that they love not their lives even unto death (Rev.12:11).

Belong to the same family – the family of God

Hebrews 2:11 says, "Both the one who makes men holy and those who are made holy are of the same family. So Jesus is not ashamed to call them brothers." As the firstborn Son, Christ is faithful over God's house (Heb.3:6). We are His house and members of God's household (Eph.2:19).

The prospective God's sons are chief sons in God's house. As such, they have greater maturity in expressing, manifesting and demonstrating the Father and have greater anointing, authority and dominion in the spirit domain.

Being made perfect through suffering

The Pattern Son was made perfect through suffering (Heb.2:10). He shared in the humanity of His brothers in order that he might become the author of their salvation to intercede for them, to help those who are being tempted, and to bring them to glory (Heb.2:14-18; Rom.8:34).

The prospective God's sons must share in Christ's suffering in order that they may also share in His glory (Rom.8:17). God uses earthly trials, tribulations, or sufferings to develop the agape love in us so that we might be matured to become His full-grown sons and be transformed to conform to the image of His firstborn Son.

Sharing in the same heavenly priesthood

Under the Old Covenant, Aaron and his brothers shared the Levitical priesthood. Under the New Covenant, Christ the firstborn and His many brothers share in the heavenly priesthood. The priesthood in the order of Aaron was appointed on the basis of a law of physical requirement, but the priesthood in the order of Melchizedek is appointed on the basis of the power of an indestructible life (Heb.7:16) This heavenly priesthood is more superior, permanent and indissoluble because it is according to the power of the eternal, uncreated, divine, endless and indestructible life. The prospective sons of God, sharing in the life and nature of the firstborn Son, become the body of priesthood of this highest order.

As our great High Priest, Christ offers perpetual and unceasing prayers and intercessions for the children of God. "Seeing then that we have a great High Priest who has passed through the heavens, Jesus the Son of God, let us hold fast our confession. For we do not have a High Priest who cannot sympathize with our weaknesses, but was in all points tempted as we are, yet without sin" (Heb.4:14-15). Today, the prospective sons of God offer prayers on earth which become incense before God's throne (Rev.5:8). When Christ our heavenly High Priest offers His prayers together with the prayers of all the saints on the golden altar before the throne, the joint-prayers of Christ the firstborn and His many brothers become acceptable to God and bring forth execution of God's judgment upon the earth (Rev.8:3-5).

Sharing in the same heavenly kingship

Descended from the tribe of Judah, the Lord is "the Lion of the tribe of Judah, the Root of David" (Rev.5:5). Under the

Old Covenant, kingship belonged to the tribe of Judah and priesthood was of the tribe of Levi (Gen.49:9-10; Heb.7:5). As one of the order of Melchizedek, the Lord is both priest and king — He is the kingly priest and the priestly king. This Melchizedek — a type of Christ — was king of Salem and priest of God Most High (Heb. 7:1). Hence, under the New Covenant, the prospective sons of God are both priests and kings. We are the royal/kingly priesthood (1 Pe.2:9). Christ, the firstborn of the dead and the Prince (Ruler) of the kings of the earth, has made us kings and priests to His God and Father (Rev.1:5-6).

Christ the firstborn is the King of kings and Lord of lords (Rev.19:16). He is the King and Lord; the prospective God's sons are kings and lords. They are now seated together with Christ in the heavenly realms (Eph.2:6). As kings in apprenticeship, they learn to rule, reign, govern and execute God's justice on earth and go to war (Prov.8:15; 2 Sam.11:1). One of the main apprenticeship programs to prepare them for rulership is learning to overcome Satan through prophetic warfare and intercessory prayers. These to-be kings are to know God's ordained seasons and times by discovering what God has concealed (Prov.25:2) so that through their prophetic utterance and words of command they might bring into existence those things that God has ordained and prepared in the spiritual realm. The prospective God's sons have power to speak into existence "those things which be not as though they were" (Rom.4:17).

Even though they are now given a foretaste of the powers of the age to come (Heb.6:5), the day will eventually come when the earth is fully under the rule and dominion of these sons of God. They will be seated with Christ on thrones and authority will be given to them to judge the world and to rule all the nations with an iron scepter (1 Co.6:2; Rev.

3:21;12:5; 20:4). They will even judge angels (1 Co.6:3). As kingly priests and priestly kings, they will reign with Christ for a thousand years (Rev.20:6).

Appointed as God's representative on earth to destroy the work of Satan

When the Pattern Son was on the earth, He brought in and manifested God's rule and God's kingdom by casting out demons and healing diseases (Mt.4:23-24; Lk.4:40-41). 1 John 3:8 says, "For this purpose the Son of God was manifested, that He might destroy the works of the devil." Acts 10:38 says, "And no doubt you know that God anointed Jesus of Nazareth with the Holy Spirit and with power. Then Jesus went around doing good and healing all who were oppressed by the Devil, for God was with him."

The first twelve apostles also shared in the delegated authority of Christ: "He called his twelve disciples to him and gave them authority to drive out evil spirits and to heal every disease and sickness (Mt.10:1)". Today, the prospective sons of God received the same anointing and delegated authority to be God's representatives and authorized agents on earth to uproot, tear down, destroy, and overthrow Satan's kingdom and works. The prospective God's sons will eventually bring this age to a close and usher in the millennial kingdom by advancing the kingdom of God through teaching, preaching, healing and deliverance (Mt.24:14;28:18-20; Mk.16:15-18). When Christ shall come again with the overcoming saints (the manifested sons of God) as armies of heaven, they will defeat Satan, Antichrist and all of God's enemies at the war in Armageddon to ultimately bring in the full manifestation of the kingdom of God upon this earth to commence the millennial reign (Rev.19:14-21; 20:4-6).

Call to
Sonship

MTC
MERIDIAN
TITLE CORPORATION

Page 116 living the divine
life
117 Jacob's ladder.
Lord's spirit joined
earth to Heaven, & heaven
to earth

Given the same ministry of reconciliation to reconcile the worldly sinners and the soulish/fleshly believers to God
As Christ was the ambassador of God to reconcile the world to Himself, the prospective God's sons are now made ambassadors of Christ in order to carry out the two-fold task of reconciliation: first, to reconcile fallen sinners to God; second, to reconcile soulish and fleshly believers to God.

> 2 Co. 5:18-20 NKJV (emphasis mine)
> Now all things are of God, who has **reconciled us to Himself** through Jesus Christ, and has given us the ministry of reconciliation, that is, that **God was in Christ reconciling the world to Himself**, not imputing their trespasses to them, and has committed to us the word of reconciliation. Now then, **we are ambassadors for Christ**, as though God were pleading through us: we implore you on Christ's behalf, **be reconciled to God**. For He made Him who knew no sin to be sin for us, that we might become the righteousness of God in Him.

The fallen human beings are to be at peace with God through the sin-redeeming death of Christ for forgiveness of sins. These sinners must be delivered from their sins and trespasses in order for them to be brought back to God and be in a righteous standing with Him. The gospel message that Christ died for their sins is the word of reconciliation for sinners so that they might be brought back to God and be at peace with Him.

However, Paul here also beseeched the believers in Corinth to reconcile to God as well. Even though they had been reconciled to God by receiving Christ for forgiveness of sins (5:15), they need to reconcile to God further and more fully in their living. Reconciliation is a saving process whereby the fallen human beings come into perfect harmony with God not only in their righteous standing (a change in standing from sinners to saints) but also in their righteous living as well (living a life that is in conformity to God's righteous nature and character). The immature children of God, like the believers in Corinth, are living, working and walking according to their soulish, natural, fleshly nature, which is in enmity with the righteous nature of God (1 Co.2:14, 3:1). As such, they need to reconcile further and more fully to God by continue to lay hold of God's grace and to exchange their soulish and fleshly dispositions for the divine nature through the impartation and inwrought of Christ's righteous nature into their whole being. The prospective God's sons know what it is to experience and take Christ as their righteousness so that Christ's righteous nature and dispositions could be infused and inter-woven into their being, causing them to spontaneously live out a righteous living that is in conformity with God's will and purpose.

As ones that demonstrate greater maturity in the divine life and carry greater anointing and authority in the spirit, the prospective God's sons represent Christ to minister His reconciling power to others (the sinful sinners and the immature saints) so that they might be fully reconciled to God by experiencing more fully the sin-redeeming death, life-releasing death and life-imparting resurrection of Christ. By the work of the reconciling ministry, sinners receive Christ's righteousness for justification and forgiveness of sins, and saints experience Christ as their righteousness for inner transformation and growth in the divine life to fullness of maturity.

Given the same power to bind and loose and forgive

While on the earth, the Lord's power to bind and loose was exemplified in His proclaiming of the year of Jubilee at the outset of His ministry: "The Spirit of the Lord is on me, because he has anointed me to preach good news to the poor. He has sent me to proclaim freedom for the prisoners and recovery of sight for the blind, to release the oppressed, to proclaim the year of the Lord's favor" (Lk.4:18-19). By the Spirit of God, the Lord cast out demons, bound Satan and set free those who were in Satan's kingdom (Mt.12:28-29). One typical example was a woman who was bound by a spirit of infirmity for eighteen years and was unable to stand up straight. The Lord healed her and she was free from the bondage in which Satan has held her (Lk.13:11-16).

The prospective God's sons are given the same authority to bind and loose. Jesus said in Matthew 16:19, "I will give you the keys of the kingdom of heaven; and whatever you bind (declare to be improper and unlawful) on earth must be what is already bound in heaven; and whatever you loose (declare lawful) on earth must be what is already loosed in heaven" (AMP). The work of Satan is improper and unlawful on earth, so God has decreed that through prayer, His sons should bind what has been bound in the heavens and loose what has been loosed in the heavens. The prospective God's sons could terminate whatever that is improper and unlawful on earth — diseases, sicknesses, and all kind of bondages — and germinate the work of God or bring into experiential reality whatever God has promised and prepared for the fulfillment of His will and purpose on earth.

The Lord demonstrated His power to forgive sins to the Pharisees by telling a paralytic that his sins were forgiven and he could now rise up and walk (Mt.9:2, 6). Likewise, He also delegated the same power to forgive or not to forgive to the prospective God's sons: "And with that He breathed on them and said, "Receive the Holy Spirit. If you forgive anyone his sins, they are forgiven; if you do not forgive them, they are not forgiven"" (Jn.20:21-22). This ability and authority to forgive the sins of others and the sins of one another is the high privilege and common right of every Holy Spirit-filled son of God. How we need to exercise this authority so that we might confess our faults one to another and pronounce forgiveness for one another in order to experience inner release and freedom for the transformation of the soul and renewal of the heart (Jas.5:16).

Sharing the same glorified body

The prospective God's sons will eventually share Christ's bodily likeness when He returns. "And as we have borne the image of the man of dust, we shall also bear the image of the heavenly Man....Behold, I tell you a mystery: We shall not all sleep, but we shall all be changed--in a moment, in the twinkling of an eye, at the last trumpet. For the trumpet will sound, and the dead will be raised incorruptible, and we shall be changed" (1 Co.15:49, 51-52). "But our citizenship is in heaven. And we eagerly await a Savior from there, the Lord Jesus Christ, who, by the power that enables Him to bring everything under His control, will transform our lowly bodies so that they will be like His glorious body" (Phil.3:20-21). "But we know that when He appears, we shall be like Him, for we shall see Him as He is" (1 Jn.3:2).

Being made joint heirs

The redeemed, regenerated, transformed and glorified sons of God will be God's legal heirs to participate with Christ to inherit all that God is and all that God has (Rom.8:17; Gal.4:7). To be designated as sons and heirs of God is the climax and ultimate consummation of believers' growth and maturity to become full-grown and functional sons of God.

The apostle Paul revealed the Church's high position as heirs of all things: "For all things are yours.....And you are Christ's, and Christ is God's" (1 Co.3:21, 23). Christ and God are eternally inseparably bound. Whatever God owns, Christ owns (Jn.3:35; 13:3). Sons of God, as also the Bride and the Body, are inseparably bound to Christ as one (Eph.5:30-32), so that whatever Christ owns, they own. Through Christ, sons of God are bound to God and to all that God is and all that God has. This is the basis of our inheritance in Christ.

Addendum Iv

The Paradox of Sonship : Now and Not Yet

Sonship is now and not yet. What does this mean? The following are explanations to this seemingly paradoxical statement.

Sonship has two aspects: the positional aspect and the experiential aspect. Positionally, we are bequeathed with sonship and full inheritance in Christ. Positionally, God has seated us together with Christ in the heavenly realms (Eph.2:6). When God raised Christ from the dead, He seated Christ at His right hand in the heavenly realms, far above all rule and authority, power and dominion, and every title that can be given, not only in the present age but also in the one to come. God placed all things under His feet and appointed Him to be head over everything for the church, which is His body, the fullness of Him who fills everything in every way (Eph.1:20-22). This means that positionally and legally, by virtue of our union with Christ, we are seated in the highest place in the universe, and all principalities and powers — include all earthly, satanic and demonic powers — are under our feet.

However, practically, Christ has yet to destroy all dominion, authority and power, and all our enemies (including death) have yet to be under our feet (1 Co.15:24-25). Experientially, we are sons now but not yet. We have received the full rights of sons and become heirs of God through Christ (Gal.4:5, 7), but the manifestation, demonstration and realization of our sonship has yet to come in fullness (Rom.8:19).

Sonship is a progression — from a child (teknon) to a son

(huios). We have yet to become God's full-grown sons. We might have the immediate and constant foretaste of sonship and the powers of the coming age (Gal.3:26; Heb.6:5), but the completion, consummation and full manifestation of sonship could only take place when Christ returns.

This kingdom principle of "now and not yet" is well demonstrated by the Old Testament's types and the New Testament's truth.

> • The Israelites were to take the land and drive out their enemies "little by little" (Ex.23:30). Spiritually, the believers are to experience and enjoy Christ as their "good land" little by little — by first experience the Indwelling Christ in their spirit and continue with the progressive experience of transforming work of Christ in their soul (emotion, mind and will) to eventually experience the full manifestation of the resurrection life of Christ in their body to overcome physical death.

> • The Israelites were to possess the land little by little until they had increased enough to take full possession of the land. God told them, "You will not be allowed to eliminate them all at once, or the wild animals will multiply around you" (Dt.7:22). God's full inheritance is not yet in our hands but it will be possessed little by little. Possessing our inheritance has the individual aspect and the corporate aspect. Individually, the more a believer grows in the divine life, the more he could exercise spiritual authority in increasing measure to bring salvation, peace, righteousness, healing into his personal life and to those who is under his influence (his family, workplace, community).

Corporately, the more the church (the gathering of the called out saints) grow and mature in the corporate divine life, the more they could subdue nations, overthrow kingdoms and establish God's kingdom on the earth. In other words, our ability to exercise spiritual authority and to possess our God-given inheritance is directly proportional to our growth in the divine life to become God's sons.

• God's kingdom is now and not yet. The kingdom of God has come on this earth (Mt.12:28; 16:19; Lk.11:2), and this kingdom is even now within us (Lk.17:21). We are delegated with kingdom's authority to be God's ambassadors, spokesmen and representatives on this earth (Mt.28:18; Lk.10:19). Yet the kingdom has yet to come (Mt.16:28; Ac.1:7; 2 Tim.4:1). The full manifestation of God's kingdom takes place during the millennium. At that time, the sons of God will rule and reign with Christ on this earth for a thousand years (Rev.20:6).

Because sonship (and God's kingdom) is now and not yet, we must actively engage ourselves in pursuing God's purpose and high call for our lives. Like the Israelites in Joshua's days, we must forcefully advancing the kingdom of God (Mt.11:12) by exercising our God-given authority and claiming our God-given inheritance (Ps.2:8). We must not neglect, ignore and despise our birthright to become God's fully matured sons and fully qualified legal heirs.

Our natural mind might be unable to comprehend fully how an individual believer or the corporate church grows into greater maturity in the divine life to have greater authority and dominion in the spirit domain, but we do know that sonship is a progression and requires a process of time. When the time of fullness comes, the sons of God will most assuredly come forth to express all that God is and to inherit all that God has. The Indwelling Spirit is the pledge of our inheritance unto the redemption of the acquired possession (Eph.1:14). The sealing of the Holy Spirit not only guaranteeing and securing our full inheritance, but also gives us a foretaste of what is to come. The deposit of the divine seed in our spirit will grow like the wheat in the field — first the stalk, then the head, then the full kernel in the head — until it is fully ripen. Sonship is now and not yet; yet the *not yet* is nearer and closer now than it was before. We must get ready now for the full manifestation of the sons of God. The harvest of the ripe and fully grown sons of God is at hand!

> *Mark 4: 26-29 NIV*
> *He also said, "This is what the kingdom of God is like. A man scatters seed on the ground. Night and day, whether he sleeps or gets up, the seed sprouts and grows, though he does not know how. All by itself the soil produces grain — first the stalk, then the head, then the full kernel in the head. As soon as the grain is ripe, he puts the sickle to it, because the harvest has come."*

To conclude, sonship is an organic process that begins with regeneration of our spirit and ends with the redemption of our body. Sonship is now and not yet: We are now the prospective sons of God and not yet the full-grown sons. At the present moment, we are undergoing the process of maturation in the divine life for conformity to Christ's image. In the near future, we will share in the bodily resurrection (for dead saints) or bodily transfiguration (for saints who are alive) when Christ returns to consummate our sonship.

Addendum V

Christ the Firstborn Son of God:
Its Meanings, Principles, Significance & Implications

We need a proper and balanced understanding of the twofold sonship of Jesus Christ: He is the only begotten Son of God and the firstborn Son of God. The Bible clearly reveals these two distinct statuses of Christ. As the only begotten Son (Jn. 1:14, 18; 3:16, 18), Christ co-exists with the Father eternally. The term *only begotten* in Greek is *monogenēs*, which means "single in its kind, only". Christ is of nature God, and even in His incarnation He is still essentially and uniquely the only begotten Son of God. As the only begotten, He has no brothers, for no creature could share in this pre-existent eternal status of the Son. As the eternally only begotten Son in the Godhead, Christ with the Father and by the Spirit created and brought all things into being (Jn.1:3; 1 Co.8:6; Col.1:16; Heb.1:2, 10). By virtue of His eternal relationship with the eternal Father, the Son is eternally God and eternally with God (Jn.1:1-2). The Son is so eternally one with the Father that He is called the eternal/everlasting Father in Isaiah 9:6.

However, Christ is also referred to as the *firstborn* in the New Testament. The apostle Paul speaks of Him as "the firstborn of all creation" (Col.1:15), "the firstborn from the dead" (Col.1:18) and "the firstborn among many brothers" (Rom.8:29). What exactly does Paul mean when He used the term *firstborn* to describe Christ?

Meanings of the term Firstborn
The adjective *firstborn* in Greek is *prōtotokos*. The root word

prōtos, bears several meanings (Thayer's Lexicon):

- first either in time or place, in any succession of things or of persons
- first in rank, influence, honor; chief; principal
- first, at the first

The term *firstborn* connotes the notion of birth. When applying the term firstborn to *all creation*, *the dead* and *many brothers*, it suggests that Christ's status as firstborn obviously refers His humanity (For Christ's in His eternal status as the Son of God in His divinity is the Creator, would never taste death, and has no brother). In Acts 13:33-34 Paul speaks of Christ's resurrection as God's begetting His resurrected humanity. We may thus deduce that the term *firstborn* is used by Paul to indicate Christ's resurrected humanity (not His incarnation).

> *Acts 13:33-34 NKJV*
> *God has fulfilled this for us their children, in that He has raised up Jesus. As it is also written in the second Psalm: 'You are My Son, Today I have begotten You.' And that He raised Him from the dead, no more to return to corruption, He has spoken thus: 'I will give you the sure mercies of David.'*

> *Romans 1:3-4 RVS*
> *The gospel concerning his Son, who was descended from David according to the flesh and designated Son of God in power according to the Spirit of holiness by his resurrection from the dead, Jesus Christ our Lord.*

According to Romans 1:4 also, Christ's resurrection from the dead was a designation, a declaration, an appointment, an ordination, a marking out. This designation is the new status that Christ gained after He rose from the dead. We know that this designation could not refer to His eternal status as the only begotten Son of God. Christ in His divinity is the Son of God in eternity — from eternity past to eternity future — and from the very beginning he was already co-existed with the Father. Acts 13:33, Hebrews 1:5 and Romans 1:4 speaks of a time in history when the Father begetting Christ in His humanity and designated Him as the Firstborn Son of God. This begetting and designating took place in His resurrection. He was designated, declared, appointed, ordained and marked out by the Father as the firstborn Son of God out of the resurrection of the dead in order that He might carry out and accomplish God's purpose of gaining His many sons. As the firstborn Son, He could now become the prototype and the pattern Son to produce the many sons of God. We too, will be the designated sons of God in full when we share in Christ's inward nature and outward likeness and are made exactly like the firstborn Son of God.

Therefore, Christ's humanity is brought into sonship through His resurrection from the dead. As a resurrected man, Christ has a new status, a new title and a new designation: the firstborn Son. This status, title and designation of Christ as the firstborn in His resurrection is of great importance if we want to see the significance and understand the meaning of the terms "the firstborn of all creation", "the firstborn from the dead" and "the firstborn among many brothers".

Principles of the Firstborn
Of equal importance, we must understand the principles of firstborn as revealed in the holy Word of God.

First, the firstborn belongs to God. According to the laws, the firstborn of man or beast and the first of the crops and fruit that ripened must be set aside, consecrated or devoted to God (Ex.13:2; 34:19; Lev. 27:26; Nu.3:13). Thus, all the firstborn are consecrated and sanctified for the Lord's purpose (Lk.2:23).

Second, God uses the firstborn to deliver the rest. The firstborn plays a redemptive role in God's economy. In Old Testament, God used the consecration of the firstborn of Israelites to judge the Egyptians and to eventually deliver the Israelites from the ushering hands of Pharaoh. In New Testament, God uses His firstborn Son to carry out his redemptive role over the fallen humanity and the fallen creation. God also uses the church of the firstborn (Heb.12:23) — the man-son, the early overcomers, the chief sons — to represent Him to have greater authority and dominion in the spirit realm and to bring deliverance to the rest in the Body of Christ.

Third, the firstborn indicates that the rest is coming. *First* implies that second, third, etc is coming. Where there is the first there must be the second.

Fourth, the *first* governs, establishes and determines the characteristics of the rest. Romans 11:16 says, "For if the firstfruit be holy, the lump is also holy: and if the root be holy, so are the branches." Thus, the first thing is the root to govern the rest. This means that the firstborn is the pattern and the type of the rest to come. All of God's children is to conform to the inward image (share in His inward nature) and outward likeness (share in His bodily resurrection) of Christ the firstborn.

The Significance and Implications of Christ as the Firstborn

Christ is the firstborn of all creation (Col.1:15). This speaks of Christ's redemptive role over the old creation. He is the One through whom the new creation came into being. As the Head of the new creation, Christ is reconciling all things to

Himself — by transferring the old creation to the new creation through the infusion of His resurrection life and power on all things. Colossians 1:20 says, "and through Him to reconcile to Himself all things, whether things on earth or things in heaven, by making peace through His blood on the cross." Christ's redemptive death bears universal application. Its saving power is effectual to redeem both fallen humanity and fallen creation. It is through Christ that all things — all of God's creation, whether human beings or all creatures — is reconciled to God.

The fall of the first Adam brought curse, corruption and death to the whole creation (Gen.3:17; Rom.5:12; 8:20). The resurrection of the last Adam, Christ, brings life, healing, restoration, reconciliation, wholeness, redemption to the whole creation. Just as Adam's sins works universally to all creation, Christ's sin-redeeming death and life-imparting resurrection work effectually through all creation to bring peace and reconciliation. The old creation is characterized by corruption and death; the new creation is characterized by life and resurrection.

Christ as the firstborn is the *protōs*, the representative Head of the redeemed humanity/creation. He is the first man/creature that has overcome the power that reigned over the old creation — death. As the first Adam brought death to the old creation, the last/new Adam brings life to the new creation. Death reigned from the time of Adam (Rom.5:14). For as in Adam all die, even so in Christ shall all be made alive (1 Co.15:22). Just as the old creation bears the characteristics of Adam's death, all things in the new creation shall bear the characteristics of Christ's resurrection life and power.

Also, the first Adam has dominion over the creation of the previous order, Christ as the last/new Adam has dominion over the creation of the new order. By raising Christ from the dead, God seated His firstborn Son at His right hand in the heavenlies, "far above all principality and power and might and dominion, and every name that is named, not only in this age but also in that which is to come" (Eph.1:20-21). It is God's plan and intention that "in the dispensation of the fullness of the times He might gather together in one all things in Christ, both which are in heaven and which are on earth--in Him" (Eph.1:10).

By the subjection of all things under His feet, the resurrected and ascended Christ becomes the Head over all things (Eph.1:22). By the operation of His resurrected power in the present age and in the one to come, all things in the old creation will eventually be rescued, delivered and set free from decay, corruption, death and darkness. By participating in the resurrection power of the firstborn and the last Adam, all things in the old creation will undergo progressive reconditioning, renovation, remaking and restoration to become the new creation. This process of renewing, remaking, reconditioning and remaking first takes place in the fallen human beings — the highest order in the created world — in this age, follows by the rest of the fallen creation — animals, plants, earth and the first and second heavens — in the millennium age.

2 Corinthians 5:17 tells us, "Therefore, if anyone is in Christ, he is a new creation; old things have passed away; behold, all things have become new." In Adam, we share in his death and become the old creation. In Christ, we share in His life-imparting resurrection power and become the new creation. However, the becoming of this new creation is a process of time. "Old things have passed away" indicates an act continuing for a time. The word "new", kainos, denotes the new primarily in relation to quality, that is, qualitative renewal

through reconditioning, renovation and re-making. Titus 3:5 confirms that we must undergo washing of regeneration and renewing of the Holy Spirit, that is, our soul must be progressively reconditioned, renovated and renewed with the life of God to be transformed. Through this progressive renewal, Christ created in Himself one new *kainos* man (Eph.2:15). This new *kainos* man is created after the likeness of God in true righteousness and holiness (Eph.4:24).

In the coming millennium age and the eternal age to come, the rest of the fallen creation will be reconditioned, renovated, remade and renewed. The Bible calls this the times of the restoration of all things in the new world (Ac.3:21; Mt.19:28). Revelations 21:1 says, "Then I saw a new heaven and a new earth, for the first heaven and the first earth had passed away". 2 Peter 3:13 says, "Nevertheless we, according to His promise, look for new heavens and a new earth in which righteousness dwells." Again, the word *new* here in Greek is *kainos*, indicating that all the things of the previous order will be qualitatively renewed to become the new order. Eventually, through the redemptive works of the Firstborn Son and His many brothers, all of old creation is renewed to become the *kainos* new creation in eternity: New Jerusalem, new heaven and new earth. As the firstborn of all creation, He is even now sitting on the throne, saying, "Behold, I make all things *kainos* new" (Rev.21:5).

Christ is the firstborn from the dead (Col.1:18; Rev.1:5). He is the firstfruits of those who have fallen asleep (1 Co.15:20). He is the first human being to be raised from death with a resurrected glorified body. Since He is the *prōtos*, the first in time to be resurrected, the rest to come will share in His bodily resurrection also.

1 Co.15:21-23, 51-53 NIV
For since death came through a man, the resurrection of the dead comes also through a man. For as in Adam all die, so in Christ all will be made alive. But each in his own turn: Christ, the firstfruits; then, when he comes, those who belong to him....Listen, I tell you a mystery: We will not all sleep, but we will all be changed-- in a flash, in the twinkling of an eye, at the last trumpet. For the trumpet will sound, the dead will be raised imperishable, and we will be changed. For the perishable must clothe itself with the imperishable, and the mortal with immortality.

Phil.3:20-21 NKJV
For our citizenship is in heaven, from which we also eagerly wait for the Savior, the Lord Jesus Christ, who will transform our lowly body that it may be conformed to His glorious body, according to the working by which He is able even to subdue all things to Himself.

Christ is the firstborn among many brothers (Rom.8:29). He is the Pattern Son, the Prototype; His many brothers are His duplications and reproduction that share in His life and nature. By our organic union with Him, our humanity will also be brought into sonship by experiencing both the inward change to conform to His inward image and outward change to conform to His outward likeness.

Central to the truth concerning sonship is that we become sons of God through Christ the firstborn. In His redemptive and life-generating roles, Christ the firstborn Son transfers the old creation to the new creation, and enables the fallen human beings to be redeemed, regenerated, transformed and glorified to become sons of God for the fulfillment of God's eternal purpose.

Note: There are two different translations of Hebrews 1:6 which bear two different meanings concerning Christ as the firstborn: 1) "And again, when God brings his firstborn into the world, he says, "Let all God's angels worship him"" (NIV). Accordingly, this translation refers to the Son's incarnation (His first coming). 2) "But when He again brings the firstborn into the world, He says: "Let all the angels of God worship Him"" (NKJV). This translation points to the second coming of Christ. Reading in conjunction with the preceding verse (vs5), and also the view that God begetting Christ as the firstborn in His resurrection (Acts 13:33), we should understand Heb.1:6 in the light of Christ's second coming as the firstborn. Christ could not come as the firstborn in His incarnation and prior to His resurrection (He was the only begotten Son in His first coming), for He only gained the status of firstborn Son after His resurrection. According to this verse then, Christ will come as the firstborn Son (with His resurrected humanity and glorified body) in His second coming.

Addendum Vi

The Manifestation of the Man-Son

"And she brought forth a male son, who shall shepherd all the nations with an iron rod..." (Rev.12:5 Darby). [1]

In the eternity past God has a plan. His plan is to bring forth a company of mature sons. The first part of this company of sons (the firstfruits) that will soon be manifested at the end of the age is the man-son as spoken of in Revelation 12:5. [2]

From the time of Adam, for every 2000 years, there is an opportune moment, a *kairos* season, a fixed and definite time on this earth whereby God's master plan is progressively unfolded, unveiled, revealed, manifested and fulfilled. 6000 years of human history on earth have passed, and we have come to the dawn of the 21st Century. The epochal season for the manifestation of the man-son is coming. The dispensation of fullness of time is near for the age of the kingdom (the millennium) to run its course on this earth.

Every 2000 years, God takes a major administrative step in executing and manifesting His activity on earth for the purpose of bringing His eternal plan and purpose into fruition. Each 2000 years is a milestone in the outworking of God's economy to gain His many sons. It will take three successive 2000 years for the completion of God's dispensational roles and activities to bring forth His many sons to usher in a new age — the age of the kingdom.

Every 2000 years God has a "son". Adam was God's created son. Abraham was God's called out son. Jesus was

God's eternal Son and firstborn Son. And soon, before the expiry of the age of grace, God will gain His corporate son constituted by the many redeemed, regenerated, transformed and glorified sons of God.

From Adam to Abraham was 2000 years. From Abraham to the Messiah was 2000 years. And from the Messiah to the man-son is another 2000 years. We are not far from this *kairos* moment to witness the manifestation of this company of the man-son.

Each "son" plays an important economical and dispensational role in accomplishing God's eternal purpose. Adam, the first human son, was created for regeneration. Adam had human life, but God created within him a human spirit which was capable of containing and receiving the divine life.

Satan, God's enemy, came to tempt God's created son in order to frustrate and thwart God's plan. From the time of Adam to Noah, the enemy had succeeded in his endeavors to gain his own sons that conformed to his corrupted and devilish nature. In the days of Noah, sons of the evil one multiplied and ruled the earth. God sent the deluge to terminate the evil and perverse generation in Noah's days.

2000 years later (from the time of Adam), God called out a man from the Ur of the Chaldeans to become the father of many nations. This called out son was Abraham. But how would this man be a father of multitude since he did not have his own child (as he and his wife were beyond child bearing age)? God promised to give him a seed coming forth from the womb of his wife. The man believed God and he begot Isaac when he was 100 years old.

The seed that God promised was not just Abraham's seed;

it was God's seed too. Galatians 3:16 says that the seed was Christ; and John 3:16 tells us that God gave His one and only begotten Son to save the world. 2000 years later, a Messiah came forth from the womb of the Virgin Mary. From Abraham until the Christ, there were forty-two generations (Mt.1:17).

Christ is the seed of the new humanity. In His humanity, He is the seed of Abraham (Mt.1:1). In His divinity, He is the seed of God. He is the divine-human seed. Out of that seed a New Man shall come forth (Eph.2:15, 4:24). Christ Himself had said, "Unless a kernel of wheat falls to the ground and dies, it remains only a single seed. But if it dies, it produces many seeds" (Jn.12:24). After His resurrection, He comes into the believers as the divine seed to regenerate them (1 Pe.1:23; 1 Jn. 3:9). This divine seed will germinate and grow in them until it becomes a tree — the kingdom people and the Mature Church. Again, Christ said, "What is the kingdom of God like? What shall I compare it to? It is like a mustard seed, which a man took and planted in his garden. It grew and became a tree, and the birds of the air perched in its branches" (Lk.13:18-19). Christ is the Branch (Isa.11:1, Zech.6:12), the many members of the New Man is the branches of the Vine (Jn. 15:5). Out of the Divine Seed comes the many seeds; out of that Branch shall grow many branches; out of the firstborn Brother His many brothers will be brought into glory; and out the Pattern Son shall come forth the many sons of God.

Around 2000 B.C., an aged woman (Sarah) travailed and out of the dead womb came forth the promised child (Isaac). At the dawn of the 1st century a virgin woman travailed and out of the virgin womb came forth the Messiah. Since then, 2000 years had gone and passed. Now, at the dawn of the 21st century, it's that time again in the earth for the aged barren woman — the Church (who has been on earth for nearly 2000 years) to travail, to cry aloud and to break forth for the bringing forth of her many children, the man-son (Gal.4:27; Rev.12:5). Out of the spiritual womb of this barren woman shall come forth the many brothers of the Pattern Son who have been conformed to the image and likeness of their firstborn Brother (The Greek word for brother, *adelphos*, means "out of the womb, a womb-brother".)

It is time again in the earth for the impregnation. It is time again to hear the cooing of the doves to remind us that a new season of life and a divinely ordained move of God are coming to bring forth the many sons of God. The opportune time has come for the Bridegroom to whisper in the ears of His beloved:

"Arise, my darling, my beautiful one, and come with me. See! The winter is past; the rains are over and gone. Flowers appear on the earth; the season of singing has come, the cooing of doves is heard in our land. The fig tree forms its early fruit; the blossoming vines spread their fragrance. Arise, come, my darling; my beautiful one, come with me." (SS. 2:10-13).

We are now standing at the edge of a dramatic and climactic moment in history. The groaning and the birth pain of the Corporate Church will intensify as this age is coming to an end. The man-son is coming forth to bring in the age of the kingdom. The whole creation waits with eager longing for the revealing of the sons of God (Rom.8:19). Instead of looking forward to the *mansion*[3] in heaven, shouldn't we wait in eager expectation for the manifestation of the *man-son*? Dear saints, I don't know whether you will have a beautiful mansion prepared for you in heaven. One thing I do know now: We are invited to become a part of this company of man-son that will soon be caught up to the throne of God. For us to qualify ourselves to rapture as the man-son, we must pass all the earthy tests and grow in divine life to mature as God's full-grown and functional sons.

Notes:
1.Most Bible translates "a male son" as "a male child" or "a man child". In Greek, the word here is huios, means "mature son". The proper term should be "a male son" or "a man-son".

2.The woman in Revelation 12 is the Corporate Church, which consists of two groups: the man-son and the remnant. The man-son is the strong part of the Mature Church, the chief sons, the firstfruits, the early overcomers. The remnant is the rest of believers constituted as the late overcomers or the harvest. The difference between the man-son and the remnant is: the man-son is caught up before the great tribulation to the throne of God before the second coming of Christ while the remnant is caught up after the great tribulation to the air at the second coming of Christ. For a more detail discussion on the subject, wait for the release of the book containing the chapter "The Overcomers".

3.The believers are popularly taught that there are many beautiful mansions reserved for them when they go to heaven. The basis of this teaching is derived from John 14:2 which says, "In my Father's house are many mansions". Contrary to the common belief, the Lord was not talking about the many mansions in heaven in John 14:2. Mansion here in Greek is monē, meaning "a staying, abiding, dwelling, abode". This same word is used in John 14:23 whereby Jesus said, "If anyone loves Me, he will keep My word; and My Father will love him, and We will come to him and make Our **abode** *with him" (NASB). This means that the Lord and the Father will indwell those who love Him and keep His words. For consistency, John 14:2 should read as* **"In my Father's house are many abodes"**. *The Father's house here is not the literal building in heaven, but the Church as God's house, God's habitation, God's dwelling place and God's temple (1 Co.3:16; Eph.2:21-22; 1 Tim.3:15; 1 Pe.2:5; Heb.3:6, 10:21). Also, in 2 Corinthians 5:1-3, Paul refers to his physical body as "earthly tent" and his future glorified body as "an eternal house in heaven". But in the context of John 14:2, the many abodes are the many members of the Corporate Church or the Body of Christ. For more discussion on this see 'Regeneration of the Human Spirit' in volume 3 of The Sons of God series.*

To contact Billy C.S.Wong, email to **billy_wcs@yahoo.com**

The second volume of The Sons of God series is entitled **The Tripartite Man, The Fall & The Organic Salvation.**